Perspectives on Renaissance Poetry

Perspectives on Renaissance Poetry

Robert C. Evans

Bloomsbury Academic
An imprint of Bloomsbury Publishing Plc

B L O O M S B U R Y
LONDON • NEW DELHI • NEW YORK • SYDNEY

Bloomsbury Academic
An imprint of Bloomsbury Publishing Plc

50 Bedford Square	1385 Broadway
London	New York
WC1B 3DP	NY 10018
UK	USA

www.bloomsbury.com

**BLOOMSBURY and the Diana logo are trademarks of
Bloomsbury Publishing Plc**

First published 2015

© Robert C. Evans, 2015

British Library Cataloguing-in-Publication Data
A catalogue record for this book is available from the British Library.

ISBN: HB: 978-1-4725-0570-5
PB: 978-1-4725-0867-6
ePDF: 978-1-4725-0701-3
ePub: 978-1-4725-1217-8

Library of Congress Cataloging-in-Publication Data
A catalog record for this book is available from the Library of Congress.

Typeset by Newgen Knowledge Works (P) Ltd., Chennai, India
Printed and bound in India

CONTENTS

PREFACE

This book

- is intended mainly for students and general readers seeking an introduction to various ways of looking at literature, especially the poetry of the English Renaissance (also known as "early modern" poetry), which in the present book means verse written roughly between 1500 and 1670.

- tries to give approximately equal weight to each of the literary theories discussed.

- includes (unusually for a book of this kind) much attention to the classical theorists whose ways of thinking were especially important during the Renaissance, and which indeed have remained important throughout much of the history of Western culture.

- tries to explain all the theories, ancient and more recent, in language that is clear and accessible.

- tries especially to show how each theory can be used and applied in practical ways to make sense of individual works of literature.

- deliberately deals with works from a variety of genres and kinds, including *carpe diem* lyrics, country house poems, epic, epic romance, epigrams, epitaphs, epyllia, erotic poems, feminist poems, pastoral elegies, religious poems, songs, sonnets, and others.

- is designed so that individual sections can be read in isolation but also so that each section builds on the one before it, with the most general discussions placed at the beginning of the book.

- allows readers to compare and contrast practically any theory with any other theory by seeing how distinct theories would respond differently to the very same poem.

- is organized roughly by dates of the poets' births, with the earlier poets generally preceding the later ones.

- includes a significant proportion of works by women poets, some of them little known.

- includes, for the most part, texts in their entireties, so that the book constitutes a small anthology of some of the most important poems of the English Renaissance.

- includes, for the most part, modernized versions of texts, but also includes, on occasion, "old-spelling" version of texts so that readers are reminded of the kind of editing that most Renaissance poems in this book and others have undergone when they have been modernized.

- is "book-ended" by chapters at the start and finish that apply *all* the theories to two individual poems.

ACKNOWLEDGMENTS

I especially wish to thank David Avital of Bloomsbury Press for his enthusiastic support of this book and for his guidance in its preparation. Mark Richardson, also of Bloomsbury, likewise deserves many thanks. It would be hard to imagine two people more helpful than David and Mark have been. I am grateful, as well, to the various anonymous reviewers who endorsed the book and made very helpful suggestions about how to make it better.

I am especially grateful for the example of Claude Summers and Ted Pebworth, superb students of the English Renaissance, and beloved by all who know them. Among the teachers who especially excited my enthusiasm for the Renaissance, I wish to pay tribute to Robert Hinman, Alvin Kernan, Earl Miner, and Robert Whitman. I was fortunate, in fact, in all the teachers I encountered at the University of Pittsburgh and at Princeton University and am deeply grateful to them all.

My students, over thirty-three years of teaching, have often been magnificent, especially those in my Literary Criticism class, who have stimulated and challenged my own thinking. Christina M. Garner, who compiled the Appendix, is one of the very best of these. I am grateful, as well, to my colleagues, especially Alan Gribben, Darren Harris-Fain, Eric Sterling, and Elizabeth Woodworth. I am especially thankful to have had as a colleague, for so many years, Joe Crowley, one of the best and kindest persons ever—perhaps the closest I have ever come to meeting an actual saint.

My deepest affection and thanks go, yet again, to my wife, Ruth, who is full of love, laughter, kindness, and fun and who shares all these traits widely and with constant joy. Our dogs—Taylor, Martha, and Rafe (sweet-natured gentleman, goofy glutton, and loving nut, respectively)—have made our lives even happier than they already were.

My debt to M. H. Abrams (July 23, 1912–April 21, 2015) will be everywhere apparent in this text, and I hope I have adequately conveyed my admiration and respect for one of the sanest and most influential of modern literary theorists.

Finally, I would like to pay permanent tribute to the great English composer Ralph Vaughan Williams, whose works—practically every single one of them—have given me more pleasure than I can possibly explain. My life has been immensely richer because he lived.

Introduction: Sir Walter Ralegh (1552–1616): "What Is Our Life?"

Although literary theory is often considered highly abstract and intellectual and therefore remote from the concerns of "ordinary" people, any reader of a literary text inevitably uses a literary theory of some sort. Any reader, that is, inevitably makes assumptions about why and how a text should be interpreted, understood, or appreciated. Responding to a text inevitably involves applying these assumptions, whether or not we are consciously aware of doing so. One goal of literary theorists, then, is simply to encourage us to be more conscious of the assumptions we make and use when we read.

By being more conscious of these assumptions, we can not only use them more insightfully but can also consider their strengths and weaknesses, their relative advantages and disadvantages. We can consider whether and in what ways they seem valid; we can make sure that we better understand their larger implications; we can determine whether we are applying them consistently; and we can help ensure that the theory we use is a theory we have freely chosen rather than one we have merely taken for granted simply because it is practiced by others.

Studying literary theory, then, can not only introduce us to different ways of reading texts but can also encourage a fuller development of our minds by prompting us not only to think for ourselves but to make sure that we can explain why we have chosen to think and read as we do.

Studying literary theory, however, has become increasingly difficult as the number of such theories has itself increased, especially during the past century. So many theories now exist, and so many often seem so difficult to grasp, that it is little wonder that so many "ordinary" readers feel intimidated (or even repelled). Trying to make sense of a given theory, and then trying to determine how that theory can be compared and contrasted with others, are genuinely daunting tasks. Different theorists seem not only to make fundamentally different assumptions but also, frequently, to speak fundamentally different languages—languages that often seem arcane and highly abstract. It is hardly surprising, then, that many readers, when confronted with the opportunity or need to expose themselves to theory, adopt the response of Melville's Bartleby and would simply "prefer not" to.

The Abrams scheme

Understanding the assumptions that lie within and beneath various literary theories becomes much easier when we heed the advice of M. H. Abrams, himself a highly influential theorist. Abrams suggested a scheme that is both firm enough and flexible enough to make sense of just about any theory one can imagine (see his famous book *The Mirror and the Lamp: Romantic Theory and the Critical Tradition* [Oxford: Oxford University Press, 1953], pp. 3–29). By applying this schematic approach to different theories, we can better understand both how they are similar and how they differ, and because the Abrams scheme encourages a systematic approach to various theories, it also makes it much easier to remember both their common and their distinctive features. Any schematic approach, of course, inevitably involves some simplification; in the final analysis, the best way to understand a particular theorist's ideas will be to examine them with individual care and attention. The Abrams scheme, however, provides a useful way to begin the study of literary theory and to organize both the tactics and the results of our thinking.

Briefly, Abrams argues that any literary theory that attempts to be complete will inevitably make certain fundamental assumptions about several basic aspects of literature. These aspects can be called the *writer*, the *text*, the *audience*, and *reality*. To these four categories we can add a fifth: the *critic*. Any theory of literature, in other words, will tend to make assumptions about the role of the writer, the features of the text, the traits of the audience, the nature of "reality," and the functions of the critic. Moreover, assumptions in one category will almost inevitably affect, or be consistent with, assumptions in another. Take an obvious example: if a theorist assumes that "reality" is fundamentally structured by inherent or imposed differences between the sexes, that assumption will in turn affect how the theorist imagines the role of the writer (e.g., male, female, sexist, liberationist, free, oppressed), the features of the text (e.g.. progressive, conservative, experimental, traditional, flexible, rigid), the traits of the audience (e.g., men, women, repressed, tolerant, conservative, liberal), and the functions of the critic (e.g., a supporter of liberation; an advocate for previously ignored writers; a student of "male" and "female" habits of thinking and writing).

Or take another example: if a theorist assumes that a literary text is a work of careful craftsmanship, she will automatically assume that the writer will (or should) be a craftsman, that the audience will (or should) appreciate such craft, and that the critic will (or should) help call attention to the highly crafted intricacies of the text. The relationship between these other ideas and the theorist's assumptions about "reality" are not, in this instance, inescapably clear. Thus the theorist may (for instance) assume that "reality" itself is highly complex and highly coherent and that the complex, coherent text therefore reflects reality; or she may assume that "reality" is so complex as to be incoherent and that the text therefore provides either a satisfying or an illusory alternative.

The category of "reality," in fact, is likely to be the most difficult category of the Abrams scheme to understand at first. For one thing, "reality" is likely to be defined differently by different theorists: some may emphasize individual psychological "reality"; some may stress social, economic, or political "reality"; some may focus on physical "reality"; some may even question the usefulness of the category (by suggesting, for instance, that an objective "reality" does not exist). Ironically, though, even theorists who doubt the existence of any independent "reality" will still need to use the concept. However, since "reality" can be defined so differently by so many different theorists, it seems best to highlight its debated, provisional status by placing the word in quotation marks or inverted commas. Most theorists can agree that literature involves texts, writers, audiences, and critics, but disputes about the nature of "reality" (or about how to understand it, if it can be understood) are often crucial to the differences between various theories. A Freudian critic makes different assumptions about "reality" than, say, a Jungian or Christian critic. Studying literary theory often involves studying different concepts of what is most fundamentally real.

The Abrams scheme provides us, then, with a simple but surprisingly adaptable method for making sense of nearly any theory we might confront or wish to use. It offers a means of appreciating both the comparisons and the contrasts between competing theories, and it even gives us a means of studying literature itself. (Abrams assumes, for instance, that every literary work will tend to embody a particular theory of literature. We might therefore analyze a story by asking what the story implies about the role of the writer, the features of the text, the traits of the audience, the nature of "reality," and the functions of the critic.) The scheme makes it easier to grasp and remember the distinctive features of different theories, and it also functions as a tool for understanding both the most ancient and the most recent theories of literature.

Literary theories: A brief overview

In a fortunate coincidence, four of the oldest but most important approaches to literature (approaches associated with Plato, Aristotle, Horace, and Longinus) happen to align nicely with each of the four basic emphases Abrams outlines—emphases on "reality," text, audience, and writer, respectively. Many later theories respond to or echo these first four, but every theory (according to Abrams) stresses one of the four components as its *key* component. In the following brief sketches, the key component of each theory is italicized. In each sketch, the word "reality" will be placed inside quotation marks as a handy reminder that different theorists tend to define "reality" in different ways.

PLATONIC CRITICISM: Because Plato prizes an accurate, objective understanding of "*reality*," he sees "creative" writers and "literary" texts as potential distractions since they may lead the already-emotional audience to neglect proper pursuit of philosophical truth, which the critic should seek, explain, and defend by using logic and reason.

ARISTOTELIAN CRITICISM: Because Aristotle values the *text* as a highly crafted complex unity, he tends to see the author as a craftsman, the audience as capable of appreciating such craftsmanship, the text as a potentially valuable means of understanding the complexity of "reality," and the critic as a specialist conversant with all aspects of the poetic craft.

HORATIAN CRITICISM: Because Horace emphasizes the need to satisfy a diverse *audience*, he tends to see the author as attempting to please and/or teach them, the text as embodying principles of custom and moderation (so as to please the widest possible audience), "reality" as understood in traditional or conventional terms, and the critic as a fatherly advisor who tries to prevent the author from making a fool of himself.

LONGINIAN CRITICISM: Because "Longinus" (whose real identity is unknown) stresses the ideally lofty nature of the sublime (i.e., elevated) *author*, he tends to view the text as an expression of the author's power, the audience as desiring the ecstasy a great author can induce, social "reality" as rooted in a basic human nature that everywhere and always has a yearning for elevation, and the critic as (among other things) a moral and spiritual advisor who encourages the highest aspirations of readers and writers alike.

TRADITIONAL HISTORICAL CRITICISM: Because traditional historical critics tend to emphasize the ways social "*realities*" influence the writer, the writer's creation of a text, and the audience's reactions to it, they stress the critic's obligation to study the past as thoroughly and objectively as possible to determine how the text might have been understood by its original readers.

THEMATIC CRITICISM: Because thematic critics stress the importance of ideas in shaping social and psychological "*reality*," they generally look for the ways those ideas are expressed by (and affect) the texts that writers create. They assume that audiences turn to texts for enlightenment as well as entertainment, and they often argue either that writers express the same basic ideas repeatedly or that the evolution of a writer's thinking can be traced in different works.

FORMALIST CRITICISM: Because formalists value the *text* as a complex unity in which all the parts contribute to a rich and resonant effect, they usually offer highly detailed ("close") readings intended to show how the work achieves a powerful, compelling artistic form. Formalist critics help audiences appreciate how a work's subtle nuances contribute to its total effect.

PSYCHOANALYTIC CRITICISM: Freudian or psychoanalytic critics emphasize the key role of the human mind in perceiving and shaping "*reality*" and believe that the minds of writers, audiences, and critics are highly complex and often highly conflicted (especially in sexual terms, and particularly in terms of the moralistic "superego," the rational ego, and the irrational "id"). They contend that such complexity inevitably affects the ways texts are written and read. The critic, therefore, should analyze how psychological patterns affect the ways texts are created and received.

ARCHETYPAL OR "MYTH" CRITICISM: Because archetypal critics believe that humans experience "*reality*" in terms of certain basic fears, desires, images (symbols), and stories (myths), they assume that writers will inevitably employ such patterns; that audiences will react to them forcefully and almost automatically; and that critics should therefore study the ways such patterns affect writers, texts, and readers.

MARXIST CRITICISM: Because Marxist critics assume that conflicts between economic classes inevitably shape social "*reality*," they emphasize the ways these struggles affect writers, audiences, and texts. They assume that literature will either reflect, reinforce, or undermine (or some combination of these) the dominant ideologies (i.e., standard patterns of thought) that help structure social relations. Marxist critics study the complex relations between literature and society, ideally seeking to promote social progress.

STRUCTURALIST CRITICISM: Because structuralist critics assume that humans structure (or make sense of) "*reality*" by imposing patterns of meaning on it, and because they assume that these structures can only be interpreted in terms of the codes the structures embody, they believe that writers will inevitably rely on such codes to create meaning, that texts will inevitably embody such codes, and that audiences will inevitably use such codes to interpret texts. To understand a text, the critic must be familiar with the systematic codes that shape it; he must master the system(s) the text implies.

FEMINIST CRITICISM: Because feminist critics assume that our experience of "*reality*" is inevitably affected by categories of sex and gender (such as divisions between male and female, heterosexual and homosexual, etc.), and because they assume that (heterosexual) males have long enjoyed dominant social power, they believe that writers, texts, and audiences will all be affected (usually negatively) by "patriarchal" forces. The critic's job will be to study (and even attempt to counteract) the impact of patriarchy.

DECONSTRUCTION: Because deconstructive critics assume that "*reality*" cannot be experienced except through language, and because they believe that language is inevitably full of contradictions, gaps, and dead-ends, they believe that no writer, text, audience, or critic can ever escape from the unsolvable paradoxes language embodies. Deconstruction therefore undercuts the hierarchical assumptions of any other critical system (such as structuralism, formalism, Marxism, etc.) that claims to offer an "objective," "neutral," or "scientific" perspective on literature.

READER-RESPONSE CRITICISM: Because reader-response critics assume that literary texts are inevitably interpreted by individual members of the *audience* and that these individuals react to texts in ways that are sometimes shared, sometimes highly personal (and sometimes both at once), they believe that writers exert much less control over texts than we sometimes suppose, and that critics must never ignore the crucial role of audience response(s).

DIALOGICAL CRITICISM: Because dialogical critics assume that the (worthy) *text* almost inevitably embodies divergent points of view, they believe that elements within a text engage in a constant dialogue or give-and-take with other elements, both within and outside the text itself. The writer, too, is almost inevitably engaged in a complex dialogue, through the text, with his potential audience(s), and the sensitive critic must be alert to the multitude of voices a text expresses or implies.

NEW HISTORICISM: Because new historicist critics assume that our experience of "*reality*" is inevitably social, and because they emphasize the ways systems of power and domination both provoke and control social conflicts, they tend to see a culture not as a single coherent entity but as a site of struggle, negotiation, or the constant exchange of energy. New historicists contend that no text, audience, or critic can stand apart from contemporary (i.e., both past and present) dynamics of power.

MULTICULTURAL CRITICISM: Because multicultural critics emphasize the numerous differences that both shape and divide social *"reality,"* they tend to see all people (including writers, readers, and critics) as members of sometimes divergent, sometimes overlapping groups. These groups, whether relatively fluid or relatively stable, can include such categories as races, sexes, genders, ages, and classes, and the critic should explore how such differences affect the ways literature is both written and read.

POSTMODERNISM: Postmodernists are highly skeptical of large-scale claims that objective "truths" exist. They thus doubt the validity of "grand narratives" or all-encompassing explanations. They see such claims as attempts to impose order on a *"reality"* that is, almost by definition, too shifting or fluid to be pinned down. Postmodernists assume that if writers, readers, and audiences abandoned their yearning for such order, they would more easily accept and enjoy the inevitable paradoxes and contradictions of life and art. The postmodern critic will look for (and value) any indications of a text's instabilities or peculiarities.

ECOCRITICISM: Ecocritics stress the importance of nature, or physical *"reality"* and its impact on writers, readers, texts, and the functions of critics. Any human associated with the production or reception of literature necessarily has crucial relations, of one sort or another, with nature. Those relations can either be positive or negative, and humans in particular can have either good or bad impacts on their environments. Texts almost inevitably reflect, either explicitly or implicitly, a range of attitudes toward nature. Ideally, texts should help promote a healthy relationship between humans and the environment, and critics should examine precisely how that relationship is depicted or implied.

DARWINIAN CRITICISM: Darwinian critics assume that human beings and all other living things are the result of billions of years of the *"reality"* of physical evolution. Because human beings share a common evolutionary history, they share many ways of thinking, feeling, and behaving that are hardwired into their genes. Literature is therefore influenced (in the ways it is created, structured, and received) by the numerous psychological traits humans share. Critics should explore the ways literature is shaped by these traits and also the ways literature can help contribute to or detract from evolutionary "fitness."

Applying the theories: Sir Walter Ralegh's "What is our life?"

Sir Walter Ralegh (1552–1618) is one of the most famous of all persons who lived during the "English Renaissance" of the sixteenth and seventeenth centuries. A courtier, explorer, historian, and highly public figure, Ralegh was also, like many other influential people of his day, an amateur poet. His lyric beginning "What is our life?" is at once brief, highly accessible, and quite representative of "early modern" literature in its themes and attitudes. For all these reasons, it provides a good test case for suggesting, very quickly, how the various literary theories can be used to interpret a single work.

WHAT IS OUR LIFE?

What is our life? a play of passion;
Our mirth the music of division;
Our mothers' wombs the tiring-houses be
Where we are dressed for this short comedy.
Heaven the judicious sharp spectator is,   [5]
That sits and marks still who doth act amiss;
Our graves that hide us from the searching sun
Are like drawn curtains when the day is done.
Thus march we, playing, to our latest rest,
Only we die in earnest—that's no jest.   [10]

PLATO admired literature that taught valuable ethical lessons. He also felt that irrational passions should be suppressed or controlled by reason so that humans could live morally worthy lives. He might therefore admire Ralegh's poem, which emphasizes the need to view life from a larger, timeless perspective. The poem also implies, especially in lines 5–6, that our lives are constantly being witnessed and judged by God, the source and arbiter of everything that is good, true, virtuous, and reasonable. God also (Ralegh suggests) will ultimately assess whether our lives have met his exacting standards. Death is inevitable, and so (the poem suggests) will be the rewards or punishments God will mete out to each of us. For all these reasons, Plato might admire Ralegh's poem for implicitly reminding us of the need to use our limited earthly time wisely and virtuously. Although Plato obviously was not a Christian, he was widely admired during the Renaissance as a "virtuous pagan" who shared and rationally justified many of the ethical values that Christians prized.

ARISTOTLE valued literature in ways and to a degree that Plato did not. He was concerned not only with the "content" of literature but also with its "form." In other words, what a literary work merely "said" was less important to him than *how* a work was structured and phrased. He was especially concerned with the complex unity of literary texts. Aristotle might notice, for instance, that Ralegh's poem begins with a question and then immediately provides a general answer to the question just posed. The rest of the poem is essentially an elaboration of the second half of line 1. The poem thus exhibits great unity. It develops an extended metaphor that compares human lives to staged dramas. Developing a metaphor over so many lines, and doing this convincingly, required the kind of literary craftsmanship and skill that Aristotle greatly admired in the best writers. He believed that the ability to coin effective metaphors was one of the greatest intellectual gifts a talented writer could possess. The ability to see a convincing resemblance between two apparently different things implied real insight, on the writer's part, into the very nature of things. In this sense the talented writer was himself a kind of philosopher. Aristotle would almost surely admire this poem for reasons too numerous to list entirely. Some of those reasons, however, would include its genuine insight into human nature and the human condition, its appropriately clear diction, and the way it begins with an abrupt question and (in a nice bit of symmetry) ends with an abrupt final quip.

HORACE, the great Roman poet and critic, argued that writers should first and foremost remember their obligations to satisfy their readers. They should use accessible, clear language, should achieve a kind of unity in their works that was not especially difficult to perceive, and should seek to teach, to please, or to do both at once. Ralegh's poem meets all these Horatian criteria. Its phrasing is lucid and simple; it teaches a lesson that is valuable partly because it accords with common sense and traditional wisdom; and it speaks of and to all humans, as if our similarities are far more important than any differences. It communicates old ideas in a fresh and witty way, and it does so in phrasing and structure that would pose few if any problems to most readers.

LONGINUS, like almost all the ancient theorists (especially Plato) valued writing and speaking that promoted virtue and other lofty ideals. He particularly prized language that was itself lofty, inspiring, and almost irresistible in its force. A great piece of writing, for Longinus, should be almost as powerful as a bolt of lightning. Ralegh's poem is not, in this sense, an ideal Longinian text. Its tone is understated and witty rather than overwhelmingly forceful. This poem does not leave us feeling, perhaps, as if we have experienced an epiphany or moment of blinding insight. Rather, it leaves us feeling persuaded by the clever analogies it draws, although the final three words do pack a slight emotional punch.

TRADITIONAL HISTORICAL critics try to establish the truth about a literary work, particularly its historical contexts and how those contexts help determine the work's meanings. Especially in dealing with any texts from the sixteenth and seventeenth centuries, a traditional historical critic might seek answers to such questions as these: What evidence is there for the authorship of the work? How can we be sure that the text we are reading is the text the author intended us to read? When was the text written? What was happening in the author's life, and in the culture at large, at the time the text was written? How might the author's life and time have influenced the content and meaning(s) of the text? "What is our life?" is often dated to around 1612—a time in Ralegh's own life when he was imprisoned for treason under a suspended sentence of death (a sentence that would eventually be reimposed and carried out in 1618). Thus the poem seems relevant to Ralegh's own existence and personal history.

THEMATIC critics, with their interest in the ideas implied or openly expressed in literary works, would obviously be interested in this poem. It concerns one of the most common of all themes in Renaissance literature: the theme of mutability, or the idea that nothing of or on the earth is stable or permanent. Other common Renaissance themes explored in this poem include the opposition between commendable reason and unfortunate passion; the idea that humans often behave foolishly and will ultimately be judged by God; and the idea that physical death is inevitable (although spiritual death is not). Ralegh's poem is one example of the long tradition in literature of *contemptus mundi*, or contempt for the world. Ironically, holding the world in contempt (it was believed) could help ensure a happier, more fulfilling life. "What is our life?"

raises a crucial question, and most of the poem can be read as a thoughtful meditation on a topic important both to literature and to everyday existence.

FORMALIST critics use the method of "close reading" to examine literary works in great detail as works of art. Anything that contributed to the success of this poem as a work of *literature* (i.e., as a piece of language intriguing and effective *as* a piece of language) would interest a formalist. For formalists, even the smallest details of phrasing, punctuation, rhythm, structure, etc. are potentially interesting. Among the many such details in this poem, a formalist might, for instance, discuss these:

- The attention-grabbing juxtaposition of abrupt question and abrupt answer in line 1, along with the alliteration of "p" sounds in that line.

- The way the poem instantly and repeatedly involves readers by reiterating the word "our."

- The alliteration of "m" sounds in line 2, as well as the increasingly lengthy responses to the opening question (one line in line 2; two lines in lines 3–4, then a repetition of two lines in lines 5–6 and 7–8), and the return to abruptness at the very end. The poem thus displays real structural design and symmetry. It achieves the kind of "complex unity" that formalists typically admire.

- The sustained development of a single metaphor throughout the poem and the cleverness and appropriateness of specific individual metaphors in particular lines and couplets.

- The brevity of the poem as a whole—a brevity appropriate to the theme that life itself is brief.

- The rich meanings of individual words, such as "still" in line 6—a word that can imply that God *always* watches us; that he is watching us even *now* (at the present moment); and even that he enjoys a kind of constancy or *stillness* denied to mutable humans. The word "sharp" in line 5 is similarly rich, implying that God is exceptionally perceptive but also that he has the power both to judge and to painfully punish. Likewise, the word "amiss" in line 6 carries at least two connotations: it suggests acting that is inept and behavior that is immoral or sinful. Formalists are especially interested in puns and other kinds of double or triple meanings, because such words or phrases are highly concentrated examples of complex unity and reveal the writer's skill as well as the richness of the text.

• The way the poem appropriately ends by referring to the end of life, as well as the appropriate abruptness—and paradoxical jesting—of the final phrase.

Formalists would find each word and even syllable of a poem potentially interesting. They are far more interested in how a poem "works" than in what it simply "means."

A PSYCHOANALYTIC critic might be interested in the ways Ralegh's poem both reflects and appeals to the complexity of the human mind, including (potentially) the minds of the author, speaker, characters, and readers. Using terms associated with Sigmund Freud, the founder of modern psychoanalysis, a psychoanalytic critic might argue that the poem alludes not only to the unconscious "id" (the seat of irrational behavior rooted in a desire for pleasure), but also to the conscious "ego" (the seat of reason and of rational engagement with reality) as well as to the "superego" (the seat of conscience, morality, and conformance to social expectations). The entire poem, a psychoanalytic critic might contend, is designed to appeal to the superegos and rational egos of readers so that readers will be more likely to discipline and control their ids. In other words, by reminding readers of their obligations to God and of God's final judgments of them, the poem encourages readers to rein in their passions. The poem functions almost as a rational argument; each new line strengthens the over-all analogy that compares life to a play. By the end of the poem, readers should (ideally) be persuaded not to "act amiss" lest they be ultimately punished by the "judicious sharp spectator" (5–6). In a sense, the poem encourages readers to themselves become "judicious sharp spectator[s]" of their own lives, constantly monitoring themselves so that they will not "act amiss." Paradoxically using the pleasure that poetry can provide, the poem prompts us to resist any impulse to indulge in mere or excessive earthly pleasure.

An ARCHETYPAL critic would also be interested in the ways this poem reflects experiences, desires, fears, and patterns of life common to *all* human beings, despite any differences of culture, society, class, ethnicity, gender, race, etc., or individual upbringing. Archetypal critics focus on shared human traits and responses rather than on traits or responses that are distinctive or unique. The fact that Ralegh's poem repeatedly uses the word "our" would immediately interest an archetypal critic; that word, and much else in the poem, implies that the speaker is addressing all humans. All humans, after all, have mothers, spend time in wombs, are born, grow up (at least to some degree), play various "roles" in life, have some experience of the sun, and eventually die. The poem focuses on very basic, fundamental patterns of human life and experience, and therefore the poem is relevant to practically every reader imaginable. The poem's combination of seriousness and humor might also be almost universally appealing. It is difficult to think of a person who would not find this poem "relevant" to one degree or another. It deals, after all, with two of the most important topics one can imagine: the desire to live a worthwhile life and the intense human fear of death.

A MARXIST critic, influenced by the critique of capitalism and ideals of communism associated with Karl Marx, might be particularly interested in the ways Ralegh's poem could be related to economics, especially to conflict between dominant and oppressed economic classes. A Marxist might argue, for example, that although life can seem short to any person, it might seem especially short—and nasty, and brutish (to quote Thomas Hobbes)—to people who are poor, malnourished, badly housed, and lacking the best possible medical care. Ralegh, although himself imprisoned during many of the final years of his life, was still a highly privileged individual in his culture. For much of his life he moved in exceptionally influential circles and was able to profit financially because of his social status. The mere fact that he was literate and could write clever poems distinguished him from most of the people living during his era. Moreover, a Marxist might contend that this poem does nothing to promote positive social change. It does nothing to make life—however short—a better experience for most people. Instead, the poem merely reinforces old reactionary ideas, especially belief in God. By encouraging readers to think about the next world (a Marxist might say), Ralegh's poem *dis*courages them from thinking about ways to materially improve the existence of the vast majority of humans in the only world that really matters: the present world of poverty, oppression, and exploitation.

FEMINIST criticism deals with such matters as women writers, women readers, and women's issues. It also often deals with relations between the biological "sexes" (or between and among different socially constructed genders) and with the ways females are depicted, either explicitly or implicitly, in literary texts. In responding to Ralegh's poem, a feminist critic might note, for example, (1) that the author is a male; (2) that most authors in Ralegh's era were males; (3) that women generally had little power and few opportunities in sixteenth- and seventeenth-century England; (4) that God, the crucial but unnamed figure in the poem, was and still is usually imagined as a male; (5) and that even the actors who literally performed all the roles (including female roles) in real plays of this period were males. Women are alluded to explicitly in the poem only as mothers (3). The roles of wives and mothers were some of the only roles women were widely expected to play in Ralegh's culture. To be socially acceptable as mothers, women had to be married, and marriage during this era was less a partnership than a hierarchy in which the husband played the leading role. In short, a feminist critic might say that the poem is shot through with the sexism of Ralegh's period in history.

STRUCTURALIST critics are interested in ways humans make sense of reality by seeing it in terms of interrelated contrasts—so-called binary opposites. These interlock with and reinforce one another. Structuralists are also interested in the ways readers depend on cultural codes to help them interpret literary texts—codes embedded in the text because authors draw on them as well. It is partly by using and interpreting shared codes that we decipher any piece of writing. Thus, anyone reading and understanding the present sentence can do so by having mastered various relevant codes, including the rules of English spelling, grammar, punctuation, and sentence structure. The "code" implied in Ralegh's poem consists of numerous interlocking and reinforcing pieces. Understanding this code is crucial to understanding the poem. The poem is built around a number of so-called binary opposites. These opposites might be outlined as follows, in which all the italicized terms to the left of the slash mark are similar to one another and all the unitalicized terms to the right of the slash mark are likewise similar: *life*/death; *reason*/passion; *stability*/mutability; *heaven*/earth; *God*/humans; *virtue*/immorality; *light*/darkness; *earnestness*/frivolity; etc. In the code implied and exemplified by Ralegh's poem, all the terms to the left of the slash marks are positive; all the terms to the right of the slash marks are negative. The whole point of the poem is arguably to (1) support the positive ideas, (2) criticize the negative ideas, and

(3) perpetuate the larger code, particularly by making the code seem natural, inevitable, and unquestionable.

DECONSTRUCTIVE critics might read Ralegh's poem by reexamining and showing the instabilities of the neat, tidy structures found in the text by structuralist critics. As the term implies, the purpose of deconstruction is to suggest that terms or ideas that seem to be clear, absolute opposites actually bleed into one another. Rather than *white*/black we thus have something resembling gray; rather than *solid*/liquid we have something far more complex and squishy. When examining Ralegh's poem, for example, a deconstuctor might put some real pressure on the supposedly clear distinction between God and humans. If God is real (a deconstructor might ask), then why are there so many different versions of "God"? Why could Christians of Ralegh's day not agree about their definitions of religion? Why were Protestants and Catholics killing each other over fine points of theological doctrine if they worshipped the same God and if that God had made his expectations absolutely clear? Which side—Protestant or Catholic—was behaving irrationally in the conflict? Which side was virtuous and which immoral? If God is associated with stability, why did conflicting beliefs about God create so much instability, suffering, and mayhem during Ralegh's era? A deconstructive reading of Ralegh's poem would not attempt to offer a final, definitive interpretation of the text but would, instead, seek to show the difficulties of achieving final, definitive interpretations of *any*thing.

READER-RESPONSE critics might argue that the impact and even the meaning of Ralegh's poem might vary greatly from one reader, or kind of reader, to another. For instance, Christian, conservative, or traditionally minded readers might value the poem's "message," while some readers might find the message, structure, and/or phrasing of the work to be trite or even worse. Marxists might consider the poem reactionary or at the very least unprogressive, while other readers might argue that Ralegh expresses ideas that are so sensible and so widely relevant that they function as conventional (some might say *too* conventional) wisdom. In short, reader-response critics would probably argue that the poem could provoke any one of a large number of different responses depending on the readers reading it.

DIALOGICAL critics might be interested in the various kinds of "dialogues" Ralegh's poem implies, especially its explicit dialogue with its readers (whose importance is suggested by the continual references to "our" and "we"), and the poem's dialogue with other works and with related kinds of literature. Ralegh's speaker seems to assume that he speaks not just for himself but for practically everyone else, including the poem's potential readers. The poem is effective partly because it immediately suggests that the speaker and his readers have so much in common. The speaker almost at once presents himself as *our* spokesman, addressing us but also preempting our own speech. He asks a question but then straightaway answers it himself, so that what at first seems like a dialogue becomes instead a monologue almost at once. Yet the poem is definitely in dialogue with other, similar texts, which it echoes and to which it implicitly alludes. The Christian Bible is obviously the most important of these texts; no other book had the same kind of pervasive influence on Ralegh's whole culture as the Bible did. Like almost anyone who adopts a religious perspective in a text, Ralegh's speaker implies that he speaks for, or at least on behalf of, God. Moreover, Ralegh's lyric is also part of a very long tradition of texts in the *contemptus mundi* tradition. It encourages us to feel contempt for the world, yet it does so in such a distinctively witty, light-hearted way that it both resembles and distinguishes itself from other, more obviously serious and sober texts on the same theme. And, of course, Ralegh's poem is in dialogue with the newly vibrant and recent tradition of English drama exemplified by the works of such writers as Shakespeare. Ralegh's poem takes for granted that its readers are familiar with plays. The poem was written at a time when drama was more important in English culture than it had ever been before.

NEW HISTORICIST critics claim that their approach to history is more complex than that of traditional historical critics. New historicists pride themselves on being interested in a far wider range of historical contexts than was true of older historical approaches. They especially focus on persons, events, places, or topics that might seem "marginal" or that have previously been ignored. Ethnic, racial, and/or sexual minorities, for example, are far more likely to receive examination from new historicist critics than was true in the past. The same is true of the history of common people and everyday life. Whereas traditional historical critics tended to focus on "major" events and prominent political and religious figures, new historicists can potentially examine anything that might illuminate a culture and cultural products, including (but not necessarily limited to) literature. They are especially interested in power relations and the negotiations for power that occur in every aspect of a society. New historicists might have much to say about Ralegh's poem. They might note, for instance, that Ralegh himself had become a very marginalized figure by the time this poem was probably written. At one time he had been one of the most powerful figures in the kingdom, but now he was under arrest in the Tower of London with a potential death sentence hanging over his head. Yet he was still more powerful than most persons living during his era. The poem can be read (1) as a way to console himself for his enormous loss of power; (2) as a way to regain and/or reassert at least some of that power by presenting himself as a good and wise man (not the deceptive traitor he had been accused of being); (3) as a way of reminding his accusers and enemies that their own present power inevitably would end when they died (if not before); and (4) as a way of insinuating that he had been victimized by people who had "act[ed] amiss" by falsely accusing him—people who would themselves someday be judged by the greatest Judge of all. In a sense, Ralegh appropriates the voice of God in this poem—the most powerful voice it was possible to possess in his era if others were willing to accept that one's words were godly. These are only a few ways in which the poem might potentially be read. New historicists pride themselves on considering the kinds of explanations that traditional historians, with their allegedly narrower perspectives, might easily overlook.

MULTICULTURAL critics argue that the writers, readers, speakers, and characters of literary works inevitably belong to particular kinds of groups. Sometimes these groups are fairly distinctive (e.g., men and women). Sometimes they overlap (e.g., black men and black women). Whereas archetypal critics emphasize traits people share, multicultural critics emphasize the traits that make different groups differ. Ralegh's poem seems deliberately to underplay and in fact ignore such differences. This fact is important, because it illustrates that sometimes the use of a particular critical perspective can help reveal traits a text does *not* obviously possess. Ralegh's text seems to anticipate the widest, broadest, least diverse kind of audience imaginable—an audience that ideally consists of almost all human beings. The poem does not seem to emerge from or anticipate particular kinds of groups, such as men, women, whites, blacks, gays, straights, the disabled, the able-bodied, etc. It *does* assume that there is a God, and although the Christian God was almost surely in Ralegh's mind when he wrote the word "Heaven" (5), it is hard to imagine any Muslim or Jew who would object to the message of this poem. Writing during a time of intense conflict among Christians, Ralegh crafted a poem that could speak just as easily for Catholics as for Protestants. By examining Ralegh's lyric from a multicultural perspective, we ironically realize just how little it seems (or even wants) to be a multicultural text.

POSTMODERNIST critics are highly suspicious of commonly accepted "truths" that try to offer broad, overarching explanations of complicated situations or events. Because they assume that reality is too complex and chaotic to explain easily, they typically prefer smaller, local responses to specific data rather than "grand narratives." They also tend to prefer texts that are complicated, rather than simple, in design, allusiveness, and impact. When creating art, they are not reluctant to mix and match diverse modes, tones, styles, and genres. Therefore, just as Ralegh's poem is not an especially multicultural text, so it is not a particularly postmodern text either. In phrasing, structure, meaning, and probable purpose, it is at the opposite end of the literary and intellectual spectrum from postmodernism. Ralegh's poem, after all, is conservative or traditional in practically every way imaginable. It consists of five well-ordered rhyming couplets; most of its lines consist of ten syllables in which the metrical stress is on the second syllable of each pair (a highly conventional meter known as "iambic pentameter"); and the poem offers a very conventional grand narrative indeed. It essentially reinforces standard Christian doctrine about the ultimate insignificance of earthly life and the need to obey God and focus on the life to come. Because this poem is so traditional in form, style, and substance, it is not the sort of text likely to interest most postmodernists.

ECOCRITICS are especially interested in relations between humans and nature. They are particularly troubled by the tendency of humans to exploit the ecosystem in destructive ways. Ralegh's poem does not lend itself in any obvious fashion to ecocritical analysis. This fact alone is significant. It implies that the speaker of this poem is less concerned with the material, physical world of nature than with the immaterial, spiritual existence that supposedly lies beyond death. The only element of nature explicitly mentioned in this poem is the sun (7), but the sun here is clearly simply a symbol of God. Humans have no more control over God than over the sun. Humans do dig graves in the earth (7), a fact that might suggest, to an ecocritic, that we all come from nature and return to it in the end. In the meantime, we use it—or rather, frequently *mis*use and abuse it—for our own selfish purposes. An ecocritic might find Ralegh's poem symptomatic of a long tradition in literature in which physical nature is ignored or denigrated as ultimately unimportant. Ralegh, of course, was deliberately writing a *"contemptus mundi"* poem, but contempt for the world, especially contempt for physical existence, is not an attitude ecocritics share. They do, however, believe that humans, in their egotistical desires for worldly pleasures and comforts, often wreak destruction on nature.

DARWINIAN critics, with their emphasis on the various ways in which evolution is relevant to literature, might find Ralegh's poem intriguing for various reasons. In particular, they might note that the poem's speaker assumes the existence of a common, fundamentally shared human nature. Darwinians agree with archetypal critics that a basic human nature *does*, in fact, exist. But Darwinians explain that fact by arguing that any basic human traits are the results of millions of years of evolution. Only genes that contributed to the likelihood of a person's survival to the age of reproduction were passed on to the next generation. In the past, especially, unhelpful mutations would have been slowly but relentlessly drained from the human gene pool. Ralegh's poem, despite its apparently otherworldly concerns, nevertheless has implications that might seem to promote evolutionary fitness. These include (1) encouragement of rational behavior and discouragement of irrational passions; (2) promotion of a collective view of the world and therefore promotion of social unity and a strong sense of communal values; (3) promotion of the idea that one's conduct is being constantly monitored by God and that violation of accepted social standards will not be tolerated; (4) promotion of the idea that individual human lives are limited and that people should therefore make the best possible uses of their time on earth; (5) promotion of a kind of stoic attitude toward mutability and the passage of time: since time *is* limited, there are only a limited number of ways to defeat death. One way is to have children; another is to create things, like this poem, that will pass part of one's mind, rather than one's physical body, on into the future.

1

Sir Thomas Wyatt (1503–42):

"They flee from me"; "My lute, awake!"

THEY FLEE FROM ME

They flee from me that sometime did me seek
With naked foot, stalking in my chamber.
I have seen them gentle, tame, and meek,
That now are wild and do not remember
That sometime they put themselves in danger   [5]
To take bread at my hand; and now they range,
Busily seeking with a continual change.

Thanked be fortune it hath been otherwise
Twenty times better; but once in special,
In thin array, after a pleasant guise,   [10]
When her loose gown from her shoulders did fall,
And she me caught in her arms long and small;
Therewithall sweetly did me kiss
And softly said, "Dear heart, how like you this?"

It was no dream: I lay broad waking.   [15]
But all is turned thorough my gentleness
Into a strange fashion of forsaking;

And I have leave to go of her goodness,
And she also, to use newfangleness.
But since that I so kindly am served   [20]
I would fain know what she hath deserved.

"They flee from me" is perhaps the most famous poem ever written by Sir Thomas Wyatt, an accomplished courtier and diplomat during the reign of King Henry VIII. Although Wyatt is important as a poet partly because of his seminal translations of sonnets by the fourteenth-century Italian poet Francesco Petrarca (or "Petrarch"), "They flee from me" is one of his original compositions.

PLATO, who distrusted literature because he thought it drew on and fed human passions, might distrust Wyatt's poem, especially if he believed that it undermined rational behavior. A Platonic critic might assume, for instance, that the poem glamorizes illicit sex. The poem's speaker recalls having had intimate relations with various women. He especially recalls one woman in particular, who once sought to seduce him. Clearly he found her conduct enticing. He is only frustrated now because she has moved on to greener pastures and new liaisons.

The poem's speaker is obviously ruled by his passions. He enjoyed the furtive love-making he recalls and regrets that those days are over. He is passionate, too, in his contempt and bitterness toward his former lover, and he hopes that she may someday suffer similar abandonment. Plato would undoubtedly condemn this irrational speaker. A crucial question, however, is whether Wyatt himself is satirizing the speaker (by presenting him ironically), or whether Wyatt sympathizes with him and indeed whether the speaker may even be Wyatt's alter ego. In short: is the poem ironic, or is it not? Should we laugh at the speaker, or should we sympathize with his painful plight? Many readers think Wyatt sympathizes with the speaker (and may, in fact, speak for himself by creating such a speaker). A strong case can be made, however, that the poem comically mocks and undermines the speaker and is humorous at his frustrated expense. The mere fact that the poem can be interpreted so differently would probably trouble Plato. He would probably have wished that Wyatt had unambiguously condemned passion rather than relying (if he even *does* rely) on irony. Precisely because literature *is* so potentially ambiguous, Plato usually distrusted and condemned it.

A TRADITIONAL HISTORICAL critic would respond to Wyatt's poem by trying to establish as many indisputable *facts* about it as possible. First and foremost, such a critic would want to establish with certainty that Wyatt wrote it. In Wyatt's case, establishing authorship is notoriously difficult. His poems originally circulated in manuscript. Therefore, the authorship of many works attributed to him has often been much debated. Most scholars do believe, however, that he did write "They flee from me." However, perhaps even more important (for traditional historical critics) than establishing a text's authorship is establishing its exact phrasing, punctuation, and structure. Historical critics often try to discover which *version* of a text the author finally intended. Again, with Wyatt (and with many other Renaissance poets), establishing "authorial intentions" is often difficult. Because poems *did* so often circulate in manuscript, and because authors often did *not* oversee any printing of their works, determining an author's precise, "final" intentions is hard. NEW HISTORICIST critics are much less concerned with establishing "final," "authorial" texts than are TRADITIONAL HISTORICAL critics. New historicists often argue that all surviving texts—especially ones widely read and accepted during the poet's own era—have interpretive value. In this respect as in so many others, new historicists resist the alleged tendency of traditional historical critics to simplify (by tidying up) the historical record.

One crucial historical fact about "They flee from me" is that it was first printed in a very popular "*Miscellany*" issued by the publisher Richard Tottell in 1557. In Tottell's edition, this poem and many others were altered from the versions available in existing manuscripts. Wyatt's poems, in particular, were often made to conform to developing standards of metrical correctness. Thus, in Tottell's version, an extra syllable was added to line 15 of "They flee from me." In manuscript, the line had read thus: "It was no dream: I lay broad waking." In Tottell's version, the line reads thus: "It was no dream, *for* I lay broad waking" (emphasis added). Tottell's version has the expected ten syllables but is often considered inferior, poetically, to the manuscript version. The manuscript (so the argument goes) emphasizes the speaker's surprise and bluntness, whereas the printed version is correct but unexciting. Most modern editors assume that Wyatt deliberately omitted the "missing" syllable. These are just a few of the kinds of "facts" traditional historical critics try to establish.

FEMINIST critics would have much to say about this poem and many other poems by Wyatt and other Renaissance authors.

Renaissance poetry often highlights relations between men and women, frequently in ways apparently "sexist." In "They flee from me," for instance, women are depicted almost as tame (and then wild) animals (4–6). They are "objectified"—treated less as complex human beings than as simple objects mainly meant to give the male speaker pleasure. Providing sexual pleasure, in particular, seems their main function for Wyatt's speaker. He seems deeply frustrated when the woman who seduced him suddenly abandons him; he dislikes such independent behavior. As the poem concludes, he seems to hope that she will suffer abandonment herself, becoming victim to retributive "karma."

Feminists might note that in this poem a man experiences how it feels to be treated as women are often treated—as mere disposable objects. Did Wyatt intend such an interpretation? Is the poem ironic—designed to mock the speaker rather than endorse his sexist attitudes? A case can be made for an ironic reading, not only of this poem but of much of Wyatt's "love" poetry. Many readers have been content simply to assume, however, that the speakers of such poems speak for Wyatt himself. Such readers assume that Wyatt endorses the sexism he depicts. In any case, he certainly depicts a sexism widespread in his own culture and perhaps even more widespread today. Feminists might applaud the woman in the poem for exercising surprising independence and turning the tables on the "male chauvinist" speaker.

READER-RESPONSE critics might suggest that there is ultimately no way to determine how an ideal or actual reader would, should, or did respond to Wyatt's poem. Any conceivable reader, they might argue, might respond in almost any conceivable way. A sexist male might sympathize with the speaker; a feminist or proto-feminist might find his attitudes repulsive; someone disposed to humor might find the whole situation funny; and so on. A religious conservative might be offended by the sexual promiscuity the poem seems to imply; a sexual libertine might laugh at the sexual restrictions of earlier periods of history; a gay male or a lesbian might find the heterosexual emphasis of the poem simply uninteresting. Whatever Wyatt "intended" the poem to mean when he wrote it, it became subject to other people's diverse possible responses as soon as it left his hands. The poem, a reader-response critic might say, ceased to be simply Wyatt's poem as soon as other people began to read it. Indeed, the poem could have different meanings even for the very same readers during different periods of their lives. A young man, for example, might sympathize with the male speaker, while that same man, when older, might find the male speaker immature and laughable. In short, the number of different possible responses to this poem is, for a reader-response critic, almost limitless. There is therefore little point in trying to determine the author's "intention" or the "correct" meaning of any literary text.

DIALOGICAL critics might focus on how Wyatt's poem either presents dialogue and/or is *in* a kind of dialogue with other texts. They might note that although the poem addresses no one in particular, in some ways it addresses the allegedly disloyal woman. She addresses the speaker in line 14, but the whole poem can be read as his lengthy retort to her. The bitter final lines, in particular, seem an angry response to the woman's rejection of the man she had earlier seduced. Yet Wyatt, when writing the poem, had to anticipate the response of the people who would read it. In a sense, then, even while writing he was engaged in a kind of dialogue with his potential audience(s). Their interests, expectations, and assumptions helped condition what this lyric does (and does not) say. And, if the poem happened to echo any well-known texts, even more dialogue was involved. Did Wyatt know, and/or did many of his readers know, the bedroom scenes in the anonymous late-fourteenth- or early-fifteenth-century poem *Sir Gawain and the Green Knight*? Wyatt's poem strongly resembles those scenes. In them, a woman sneaks into a man's bedroom to seduce him. Was Wyatt in conscious dialogue with that earlier poem when he wrote his own? Would his first readers have noted resemblances between his poem and *Sir Gawain*? A dialogical critic might ask these kinds of questions concerning Wyatt's famous lyric.

MY LUTE AWAKE!

My lute awake! perform the last
Labour that thou and I shall waste,
And end that I have now begun;
For when this song is sung and past,
My lute be still, for I have done.   [5]

As to be heard where ear is none,
As lead to grave in marble stone,

My song may pierce her heart as soon;
Should we then sigh or sing or moan?
No, no, my lute, for I have done.   [10]

The rocks do not so cruelly
Repulse the waves continually,
As she my suit and affection;
So that I am past remedy,
Whereby my lute and I have done.   [15]

Proud of the spoil that thou hast got
Of simple hearts thorough Love's shot,
By whom, unkind, thou hast them won,
Think not he hath his bow forgot,
Although my lute and I have done.   [20]

Vengeance shall fall on thy disdain
That makest but game on earnest pain.
Think not alone under the sun
Unquit to cause thy lovers plain,
Although my lute and I have done.   [25]

Perchance thee lie withered and old
The winter nights that are so cold,
Plaining in vain unto the moon;
Thy wishes then dare not be told;
Care then who list, for I have done.   [30]

And then may chance thee to repent
The time that thou hast lost and spent
To cause thy lovers sigh and swoon;
Then shalt thou know beauty but lent,
And wish and want as I have done.   [35]

Now cease, my lute; this is the last
Labour that thou and I shall waste,
And ended is that we begun.
Now is this song both sung and past:
My lute be still, for I have done.   [40]

In this lyric, perhaps intended to actually be sung to accompany lute music, a frustrated lover first complains about, and then somewhat darkly berates, the lady he has been trying to seduce. She ignores him (a very typical situation in Renaissance "love" poetry). Ultimately he becomes so angry that he imagines her lying "withered and old" in her bed during cold winter nights in the future. He hopes that she will then regret having bypassed having sex with him when she had the opportunity.

ARISTOTLE, unlike his teacher Plato, valued literature not mainly for what it said or meant but especially for how well and skillfully it was crafted. He would therefore find much to admire in Wyatt's poem. First, the poem deals with very common human emotions, especially the emotions of frustration and anger. It thus reveals significant aspects of human nature. Aristotle considered such revelations an important function of literary texts. Second, the poem is carefully structured. Its constant use of the same refrain only highlights the growing intensity of the speaker's feelings. Each time the speaker returns to the refrain, the poem's emotional "temperature" increases.

Yet Aristotle may also have been intrigued by the possible irony of the poem. In other words, it is possible to argue that as the poem develops, the speaker seems less and less sympathetic. At first he seems merely somewhat humorous (especially when he keeps claiming he is "done" and then starts yet another stanza). It is as if Wyatt is mocking the speaker's foolishness. By the end of the poem, however, the speaker reveals a genuinely dark vengefulness.

Irony, almost by definition, involves the kind of complex unity Aristotle admired. An ironic word, phrase, or poem has at least two meanings rather than just one—an apparent meaning and also a deeper, often alternative meaning. Successful irony is inevitably both complex and unified. Thus it appeals both to Aristotle and to latter-day formalists. To use irony effectively is to reveal genuine literary skill.

Examples of possible irony abound in this poem. For instance, in line 2 the speaker implies that he is wasting his time by courting this woman, which is true in more senses than he admits. In line 16, he accuses the woman of pride, although the poem may actually reveal his own vanity and egocentrism. In line 22, he claims that the woman enjoys seeing others suffer, but by the end of the poem he has revealed his own desire to see *her* in pain. In line 28, he almost compares the woman to a sex-starved animal—a description that more nearly fits him, at least as he reveals himself in this poem. Most arguably ironic of all, however, are lines 36–7, when he warns the woman that someday she will "repent" wasting her time. Arguably it is the speaker himself who has wasted (and continues to waste) his own time pursuing a woman who clearly has no interest in him. The poem, rather than being merely an expression of the speaker's passion, can therefore be read as humorous, ironic mockery of that passion.

THEMATIC critics are interested in the ideas literature explores or expresses, especially if those ideas are (1) important to a work's unity and/or structure; (2) typical of a particular writer's work in general; and/or (3) typical of the writer's culture or era. Among the themes that help organize Wyatt's poem (and that are also often typical of his era) are these: (1) the frustrations of earthly desires; (2) the disadvantages of wasting time; (3) the supposed cruelty of women who refuse to have sex with desperate men; (4) the dangers of pride; (5) the power of Cupid; and (6) the mutability or impermanence of earthly beauty (to mention just the most obvious themes). Some thematic critics would choose, from among these six ideas, a "central theme" or "key motif" that would subsume them all. Some thematic critics claim to have found the one key idea or *leitmotif* that makes sense of an entire work. Whether or not one would choose a "central theme" for Wyatt's poem, there seems little doubt that all the ideas already mentioned are definitely present and important in this work.

PSYCHOANALYTIC critics, with their interest in relations between the conscience (the superego), the rational mind (the ego), and unconscious passions (the id), might be particularly interested in Wyatt's poem. Clearly the speaker is driven by his passions, although he does use his reason (ironically) to try to explain and justify (rather than control and suppress) them. Ultimately, his passions seem to dominate him completely, and, in desiring to see the woman suffer pain, he arguably also loses contact with his conscience. He never finds fault with himself, but only with her. He never examines his own motives rationally or ethically; instead, he indulges in them more and more as the poem proceeds. His interest in the woman seems almost obsessive/compulsive. He seems in thrall to his own narcissistic desires. He cannot imagine that the woman has any legitimate reasons for rejecting him. He refuses to take "no" for an answer. And it is possible to argue that in line 29 he projects his own shameful desires onto the woman, imagining *her* as someday succumbing to the immoral thoughts and feelings now dominating *him*. A poem that begins by seeming amusing ends, one might claim, by revealing a far darker side of the speaker's mind than he probably intended to disclose.

NEW HISTORICIST critics are often concerned with the ways power is felt, exercised, and negotiated. Unlike traditional historical critics, who tend to focus on obviously powerful persons (such as kings, presidents, generals, popes, and other figures at the top of any social hierarchy), new historicists are often just as likely to focus on power relations at the individual or "micro-political" levels. Renaissance love poetry is often very much concerned with power relations between suitors (usually male) and the objects of their attentions (usually female). Although women in Renaissance society often possessed little real power as daughters and wives, they did possess some genuine power when they were being courted, especially if they were women of genuine social status, such as women at court. In Wyatt's poem, the male speaker protests against the allegedly heartless treatment he has received from the women he has been trying to seduce. By revealing his supposed mistreatment, he reveals his relative lack of power. However, by painting the woman as cruel, he tries to win our sympathy, break down her resistance, and thus enhance his power. His poem can be read as one move in a complicated game of social chess.

DARWINIAN critics, with their interest in relations between the sexes and particularly in males courting females, would clearly find Wyatt's poem worth discussing. The male in this poem behaves in precisely the way Darwinians might predict—and so, for that matter, does the woman. Darwinians assume that males have found it advantageous, over many eons, to have sex with as many females as they could, thus passing on their genes to as many potential offspring as possible. Darwinians assume that women, on the other hand, have long had a vested interest in finding mates willing to settle down, show loyalty, and provide for them and their offspring. Women, because they can become pregnant, have very good reasons to be choosy when selecting sex-partners. This was especially true before reliable birth control had been developed. Males, on the other hand, have little incentive to be choosy at all in seeking sex-partners, especially if those males are interested primarily in sexual pleasure and not in making long-term commitments. A Darwinian might argue that the woman in this poem rejects this speaker for several possible and very good Darwinian reasons: (1) she may suspect that his interest is mainly in sex, not in being a dependable husband and father; (2) she may worry that she will become pregnant if she has sex with him and that he will not marry her; and (3) she may worry that if she does have casual sex with him and others find out, she will not be appealing as a potential wife to a man who truly does want to get married, be faithful, and have and support legitimate children.

2

Henry Howard, Earl of Surrey (1517–47):

"Love, that doth reign and live within my thought"; "Th'Assyrians' king, in peace with foul desire"

LOVE, THAT DOTH REIGN AND LIVE WITHIN MY THOUGHT

Love, that doth reign and live within my thought
And built his seat within my captive breast,
Clad in the arms wherein with me he fought,
Oft in my face he doth his banner rest.
But she that taught me love and suffer pain,   [5]
My doubtful hope and eke my hot desire
With shamefast look to shadow and refrain,
Her smiling grace converteth straight to ire.
And coward Love then to the heart apace
Taketh his flight, where he doth lurk and plain,   [10]
His purpose lost, and dare not show his face.
For my lord's guilt thus faultless bide I pain;

Yet from my lord shall not my foot remove:
Sweet is the death that taketh end by love.

Henry Howard, Earl of Surrey is almost always paired in literary histories with Sir Thomas Wyatt. Both were courtiers during the reign of King Henry VIII, and both were amateur poets with a strong interest in translating the works of Petrarch into English. Surrey, who outranked Wyatt, nonetheless admired the older man's character and accomplishments, especially his accomplishments as a poet. The present poem, like many of Wyatt's (and Petrarch's), deals with a male's unsuccessful attempts to court a female. Cupid (the "Love" of line 1) has captured the speaker's mind and emotions (1–2), even causing him to blush (4). But the lady he desires resists his advances angrily, and he blames her for thus causing him pain (5–8). Cupid, repulsed by the lady, abandons the field of erotic combat (9–11). The speaker ends by claiming that his suffering is therefore Cupid's fault, but that he will nevertheless remain loyal to Cupid until the day he dies (12–14).

HORACE, with his interest in poetry that is accessible, traditional, and yet not slavishly imitative, would surely admire Surrey's poem. After all, Surrey's language is often contrasted with Wyatt's. Wyatt's phrasing and rhythms are often described as rough and irregular. Conversely, Surrey's are often described as smooth and disciplined. In this poem, for instance, lines sometimes begin with metrical irregularity, but almost always they shift to utterly regular iambic meter. This kind of shift occurs, for instance, in lines 1, 3, 4, 10, and 14. All the other lines are thoroughly regular to begin with. Surrey's mastery of iambic pentameter rhythms greatly influenced later poets.

The fact that the present poem, like many of Surrey's works, is a clear translation of one of Petrarch's sonnets would also please Horace. By translating Petrarch into English, Surrey was being both traditional and innovative. He was following foreign conventions while also helping to introduce those conventions into English. He was demonstrating his mastery of an important genre (the sonnet) while also innovating within that genre, particularly by adopting a different rhyme scheme than Petrarch had used. Petrarchan sonnets inevitably rhyme as follows in the "octave": abba abba. Variation is permitted, however, in the last six lines, or "sestet." Surrey's octave here rhymes as follows: abab cdcd. A third quatrain then ensues, and the poem ends with a couplet: efef gg. This is the same structure Shakespeare would later use in his own sonnets. Surrey, then, was influenced by Petrarch, altered Petrarchan example, and influenced important later writers. Yet his alterations were not radical, nor was his influence. Horace would admire both his imitation of Petrarch and the fact that his imitation was not slavish.

ARCHETYPAL critics, with their interest in the basic motives, traits, desires, and fears that all humans share, would have much to say about Surrey's poem. Nearly all humans, for instance, feel a yearning for love, and nearly all fear rejection and know how it feels to be rejected. Nearly everyone has felt dominated by desires that they seem powerless to resist or control (as this speaker feels dominated by Cupid), and almost all people resist accepting responsibility for their own irrational, passionate thoughts and behavior. Finally, practically everyone can relate to this speaker's intention, at the end of the poem, to persist in thoughts, feelings, and conduct that have already proved pointless and counterproductive. The speaker's self-deluding stubbornness in the final line is, unfortunately, an all-too-human trait. Because it deals with fundamental aspects of "human nature," Surrey's poem would definitely interest archetypal critics.

STRUCTURALIST critics are interested in the various "codes" that make a work of literature intelligible and that help dictate its meaning. The most obvious code or system of meanings relevant to Surrey's poem is the English language itself. The word "eke" (i.e., "also" [6]), for instance, is no longer a word commonly used in standard English. In order to understand Surrey's poem, we therefore need to rely on historical dictionaries and editorial notes to explain that word as well as some other phrasing. Almost as important as knowing English, however, if we hope to understand Surrey's poem, is the importance of knowing the "code" of Petrarchan sonnet writing. Petrarchan sonnets almost always feature a male who feels desperate yearning for a female. Almost always she rejects his desire for her. About this much, almost everyone agrees. But the further significance of the Petrarchan "code" is the subject of much debate. Some critics assume that we are supposed to sympathize with the male Petrarchan lovers and that those lovers are in fact simply alter egos of the authors themselves. Other critics argue, in contrast, that the male lovers are presented as negative examples—as examples of how *not* to think, feel, or behave. In other words, some critics read Petrarchan poems straightforwardly, while others think that the "code" implies and encourages an ironic response. Consider, for instance, the last two lines of Surrey's poem. Some readers believe that those lines imply an admirable continuing commitment to love. Others, however, think that those lines imply a foolish continuing commitment to the wrong *kind* of love—to "*cupiditas*" rather than to "*caritas*" (i.e., to selfish desire rather than to selfless, Godly affection). Evidence can be cited to support both interpretations of the Petrarchan "code." Therefore, interpreting any particular Petrarchan poem is often difficult and a matter of dispute.

DECONSTRUCTIVE critics would not find the difficulty of "properly" interpreting the Petrarchan code at all surprising. Instead, they would find it utterly typical of many, if not all, problems of interpreting any text. Almost no code, they would argue, is capable of dictating plain, unambiguous, indisputable interpretations. A deconstructor would argue that the Petrarchan code and Petrarchan texts, in particular, lend themselves to contradictory interpretations that can finally seem irresolvable. For example, the very first word of Surrey's poem ("Love") is open to radically different interpretations. While most commentators would agree that "Love" here refers to Cupid, many commentators would radically disagree about the significance of this kind of "Love." Is it genuine, selfless, Godly love (*caritas*), in which the beloved is the focus of true and enduring affection? Or is it false, selfish, worldly desire (*cupiditas*), in which the so-called beloved is the object of mere impermanent lust? Some interpreters might say that the woman's angry rejection of this suitor suggests that she considers his desires blameworthy and unappealing. Other analysts would say that her rejection of him is merely a convention of Petrarchan poetry. These latter analysts might say that we are intended to sympathize with the rejected suitor. Other commentators might argue that he and other such suitors are the objects of ironic mockery. Practically every key word in the text can be read in diametrically opposite ways. For instance, is the speaker's heart truly "captive" (2), or has he foolishly surrendered it? Is the woman the cause of the speaker's pain (5), or is he responsible for his own suffering? Is his loyalty to Cupid (13) something we should admire, or is it merely foolish and self-defeating? To the extent that such questions seem undecidable, the poem has been deconstructed. Or, rather, it has revealed the kind of irresolvable contradictions typical of so many texts. Deconstructors are uninterested in producing final, indisputable interpretations but in showing that such interpretations are "always already" impossible. POSTMODERNIST critics would agree with the basic deconstructive analysis of Surrey's poem. Some analysts, in fact, see deconstruction as simply one of many varieties of postmodern thought. No grand narrative or broad interpretive framework (a postmodernist might claim) can help us make final sense of Surrey's poem. Yet postmodernists might actually find Surrey's sonnet relatively uninteresting for several reasons. First, because it *is* a Petrarchan poem, it is highly conventional and almost predictable. A postmodernist might say that there is nothing very surprising, intriguing, or thought-provoking about poems like this one. Second, Surrey's poem, while slightly innovative in form, is arguably not at all innovative in substance. It is, after all, a translation of one of Petrarch's own lyrics. It is a conservative, traditional text for that reason alone. Almost by definition, this poem does not mix genres in the ways postmodern critics often prize. Nor is there much evidence in this work of any contact with genuinely popular culture. Petrarchan poems appealed especially to aristocrats, courtiers, and other literate people of the time. Very few "common" people were reading or writing Petrarchan sonnets. Surrey's poem would be far more interesting to a postmodernist if it interacted more obviously with elements of the popular culture of the period—the kind of culture rarely represented in anthologies of Renaissance literature and rarely discussed by students of Renaissance culture.

TH'ASSYRIAN'S KING, IN PEACE WITH FOUL DESIRE

Th'Assyrians' king, in peace with foul desire
And filthy lust that stained his regal heart,
In war, that should set princely hearts afire,
Vanquished did yield for want of martial art.
The dint of swords from kisses seemèd strange,   [5]
And harder than his lady's side, his targe;
From glutton feasts to soldier's fare, a change,
His helmet, far above a garland's charge.
Who sca[r]ce the name of manhood did retain,
Drenchèd in sloth and womanish delight,   [10]

Feeble of sprite, unpatient of pain,
When he had lost his honor and his right
(Proud, time of wealth; in storms, appalled with dread),
Murdered himself, to show some manful deed.

The "Assyrian king" described in Surrey's poem is Sardanapalus, legendary for behavior that most people in Surrey's day considered decadent self-indulgence. He is supposed to have dressed like a woman and to have had both male and female lovers. Attacked by rebels and their allies, he eventually killed himself to prevent capture and execution. There seems to have been no actual king of ancient Assyria named Sardanapalus, but his existence was widely assumed in Surrey's day.

LONGINUS believed that literature should ideally spring from and encourage the highest, noblest aspects and aspirations of human nature. The best literature should and would reflect the lofty, sublime character of the writer and should inspire such loftiness in readers. Surrey's poem arguably achieves these goals by presenting an ironic example of an *i*gnoble, repulsive figure. Precisely because Sardanapalus was a king, he would have been especially obligated (according to a Christian aristocrat such as Surrey) to set a moral, uplifting example for his people. As a ruler, he in particular should have rejected materialism, selfishness, immorality, and obsession with worldly goods and worldly pleasure. Surrey, by depicting such a corrupt and corrupting figure, implicitly teaches us how *not* to behave, how *not* to live our lives. A Longinian critic might argue that Surrey in this poem tries to inspire us both to be good and to do good by showing as a ruler who tried to do neither. Presumably, only a person of lofty moral character would be inspired to write a poem so strongly condemning such an obviously immoral ruler as Sardanapalus.

FORMALIST critics would be less interested in the paraphraseable meaning of this poem than it is skill and effectiveness as a work of art. Formalists prize "close reading," the method of examining practically every detail of a work to determine how all those details contribute to the unity and impact of the whole poem. In responding to Surrey's sonnet, formalists might make observations such as the following:

- Almost the entire poem follows a highly regular iambic pentameter rhythm (i.e., with accents mainly on the even-numbered syllables). This means that any words that break this pattern receive special emphasis. Such words include "Vanquished" (4) "Drenchèd" (10), and, especially, "Murdered" (14). Not surprisingly, all these words are verbs or action-words, but "Murdered" is especially and effectively emphatic because it catches us so much by surprise.

- The phrasing in general is clear, simple, and straightforward. Most of the words are of Anglo-Saxon origin rather than stemming from Latin roots, and many of them are emphatically monosyllabic.

- The sentence structure is also simple: single nouns are often paired with single adjectives (e.g., "foul desire"; "filthy lust"; "regal heart"), giving the poem a strong sense of balance and organization. This is especially true in the first four lines, which particularly balance the phrases "in peace" (1) and "In war" (4).

- Lines 5–8 are structured around a series of balanced opposites, especially "swords" and "kisses" (5), "side" and "targe" (i.e., shield [6]), "glutton feasts" and "soldier's fare" (7), and "helmet" and "garland" (8). The clear structure of the poem and its lucid, balanced phrasing suggests that the speaker, unlike Sardanapalus, is both disciplined and rational.

- The speaker shows a real sensitivity to sound effects, as in the use of alliteration of "d" and "s" sounds in line 5 and the repeated "ar" sounds in lines 6 and 8 (to mention just two examples).

- Finally, a formalist might note the long, dependent structure of lines 9–14, in which the main verb ("Murdered") is delayed and delayed until finally, when it arrives, it achieves maximum impact, partly because the first syllable is stressed and partly because it comes at the very beginning of a new line.

MARXIST Marxist critics, with their interest in relations between oppressors and the oppressed, would have much to say about Surrey's poem. They might argue, for instance, that Sardanapalus could never have been as phenomenally and influentially corrupt if he had not been a king or if he had lived in a society in which everyone was socially and economically equal. His great political and economic power allowed him to abuse his subjects and to profit, unfairly, from their labor. His values were essentially selfish and materialistic. He cared about no one other than himself. In that sense, he was typical of most people in most ruling classes during most of human history. The death of Sardanapalus did not end oppression in his society; it only allowed oppression to continue under new rulers and new members of a corrupt elite. Only a fundamental change (a Marxist might say)—indeed, only a communist revolution—can usher in a new kind of society in which people such as Sardanapalus can no longer arise. (Of course, the fact that such people have indeed arisen and flourished in communist societies—think of Stalin or Mao or Pol Pot—complicates this claim.)

FEMINIST critics might note the way women are depicted in this poem and how those depictions help contribute to the negative stereotypes about women that have flourished in many cultures for thousands of years. Thus, in line 6 a woman is presented as one of the many sensual pleasures that helped distract Sardanapalus from his proper manly duties as a king. The "lady" mentioned in that line resembles the Biblical Eve in the sense that all women who sin or "cause" sin have traditionally been treated in Western culture as the daughters of Eve. Sardanapalus dressed in ways conventionally associated with women (8). He failed to behave in the ways conventionally associated with men (9). He succumbed to "womanish delight" (10). And, finally, he committed suicide to demonstrate at least one "manful deed" (14). In short, throughout the poem, women are symbolically associated with sin and weakness. Or perhaps it is more accurate to say that sin and weakness are described in "womanish" terms. In either case, women in this poem are cast in a negative light, and Sardanapalus becomes a figurative woman because he fails to act like a proper man. Feminists might argue that language such as the language of this poem—which resembled language used throughout the Renaissance, as well as before and after—helped contribute to the deep-seated sexism of much of Western culture.

MULTICULTURAL critics might note the various alternative cultures or subcultures implied in this poem and how the poem's references to those groups might promote prejudice against them. The sexism that might be alleged against the poem has already been mentioned. Yet the poem may also have contributed to the long Western tradition of homophobia, or prejudice against homoerotic behavior. To the extent that Sarndanapalus was famous for having sex with other men and was condemned for doing so, this poem and writings like it might contribute to a widespread hatred of gay people that continues to this day (particularly in non-Western countries). Perhaps the reference to "filthy lust" (2) is an oblique allusion to the king's sex with other men. The fact that he allegedly gave in to "womanish delight" and that he was "Feeble of sprite, [and] unpatient of pain" (9–10) would have made him sound, to many Renaissance and later readers, repulsively effeminate. The poem might thus feed prejudice against persons who fail(ed) to conform to standard expectations of "proper" male and female behavior. Yet the poem can also be read as an example of a long Western prejudice against non-Christians in general and middle-eastern "heathens" in particular. People in the Renaissance would probably have associated Sardanapalus and the Assyrians with middle-eastern Muslims of their day, with whom European Christians had been at war for centuries. The Middle East was often associated, in the minds of many Westerners, with the kind of "Oriental despotism" Sardanapalus seems to symbolize. Multicultural critics would be sensitive to any tendency of literary texts to foment prejudice against any kind of group regarded as fundamentally different, alien, distinct, and (almost inevitably) inferior.

3

Anne Vaughan Locke (1534?–after 1590):

"And then not daring with presuming eye"; "Have mercy, God, for thy great mercy's sake"

Anne Vaughan Locke is now widely believed to be the author of a series of religious sonnets published in 1560 (without specific attribution) as an appendix to her translation of a series of sermons by John Calvin (1509–64). Calvin, a French theologian, was one of the most important figures of the Reformation, the definitive break of various kinds of "Protestants" from the Roman Catholic Church. This break was one of the most important events in European history. It had an enormous impact on the political and religious history of England, especially in the sixteenth century. Henry VIII (1491–1547) was at first a Catholic but then broke from the church because the Pope refused to allow him to divorce his first wife. (Henry had come to believe, or at least claim, that their marriage was illegitimate in the eyes of God.) Henry's son and successor, the young Edward VI (1537–53) was a genuinely devout Protestant. When he died prematurely, however, his half-sister Mary I (1516–58) became queen. She was a devout Catholic and tried to restore (or reimpose) the Catholic faith in England. When she in turn died, she was succeeded by *her* half-sister, Elizabeth I (1533–1603), a moderate Protestant who undid many of the changes Mary had wrought. In short, Anne Vaughan Lock was living in times of great religious flux. Her prose and poems reflect her deep commitment to Protestant Calvinism.

The sonnets now commonly attributed to Locke are titled *A Meditation of a Penitent Sinner*. They constitute the first known "sonnet sequence" in English—the first attempt to sustain a continuing narrative in a collection of English sonnets. The first five of Locke's sonnets are prefatory works; the remaining twenty-one are paraphrases, in verse, of Psalm 51—one of the so-called Penitential Psalms. The first five sonnets are very tightly linked to one another, as are the remaining twenty-one. "And then not daring with presuming eyes" is the fifth of the five prefatory sonnets. Mainly for the sake of convenience, but also because this poem probably does reflect views and feelings Lock herself would readily embrace, the speaker of the poem will be assumed here to be a female.

AND THEN NOT DARING WITH PRESUMING EYE

And then not daring with presuming eye
Once to beholde the angry heauens face,
From troubled sprite I send confused crye,
To craue the crummes of all sufficing grace.
With foltring knee I fallyng to the ground,   [5]
Bendyng my yelding handes to heauens throne,
Poure forth my piteous plaint w[ith] woefull sound,
With smoking sighes, & oft repeted grone,
Before the Lord, the Lord, whom synner I,
I cursed wretch, I haue offended so,   [10]
That dredyng, in his wrekefull wrath to dye,
And damned downe to depth of hell to go,
Thus tost with panges and passions of despeir,
Thus craue I mercy with repentant chere.

PLATO, or critics influenced by him, might admire the speaker of this poem for the deep concern she expresses for proper moral behavior.

She has a highly developed conscience and seems greatly troubled by the thought that she has fallen short of God's expectations and desires. Rather than trying to deny her imperfections or explain them away, she readily admits to being a sinner. She has a strong sense of her own subordinate place in the hierarchy of the universe. She readily concedes her obligations to behave morally and righteously. For all these reasons, she would make a good citizen in the kind of moral commonwealth Plato envisaged in his highly influential book *The Republic*. Lock's speaker here displays a strong sense of spiritual responsibility and accountability.

On the other hand, Plato or his followers might be troubled by the intensity of the speaker's passion. Rather than responding rationally to her sense of sinfulness, she often seems overwrought and out of emotional control. She might, paradoxically, even be vulnerable to accusations of egotism. She mentions herself repeatedly, so that what might otherwise have seemed humility can in some ways be viewed as narcissism. Plato would surely admire her deep-seated desires to be morally and spiritually worthy, as well as her unquestioned willingness to confess her flaws. The heated emotional tone of the poem, however, might cause Platonic critics some real misgivings.

TRADITIONAL HISTORICAL critics might argue that the tone and diction of this poem were not at all unusual in Calvinist writings of Locke's day. What seems exceptionally and personally emotional to present readers might have struck Locke's original audiences as simply typical of the way many Calvinists at the time expressed themselves. Certainly a traditional historical critic would want to examine as much evidence as possible from the period to determine if this was indeed the case. Such a critic would want, in particular, to study other writings by Locke, especially other poems, to determine if the tone and phrasing used here were typical of her ways of expressing herself. Clearly, too, a traditional historical critic would want to seek for even firmer evidence than has already been found that Locke herself was the author of these poems. At present, the evidence supporting her authorship is mainly circumstantial and inferential. A traditional historical critic would welcome any hard, indisputable evidence either confirming or disconfirming that Locke was the person who wrote these poems. Such evidence might include a manuscript version of the poems in her own handwriting, a contemporary letter or letters attributing the poems to Locke, or any other documentary confirmation that Locke did indeed write the sonnets for which she is now widely given credit.

PSYCHOANALYTIC critics might find in this poem strong evidence of all three basic aspects of the mind as they were identified by Sigmund Freud. That is, the poem reveals the existence of the speaker's superego (or conscience), her ego (or rational sense of personal identity), and her id (or the wellspring of her deepest fears and desires). However, rather than showing how the superego keeps the ego and id under control, this poem may in fact reveal how the superego can inflame the ego and id. Or, rather, it may show how the id can distort and exaggerate the moral impulses associated with the superego. A psychoanalytic critic might argue that the speaker of this poem has developed an irrational fixation on her own sinfulness. She may seem to have been driven almost to the point of madness by her conviction that she is unworthy. She might even be diagnosed as having an abnormal fixation on God as a wrathful, punishing judge rather than as a merciful heavenly father. Her phrasing might, to a Freudian, seem overblown and melodramatic. And, even if her attitudes were typical of Calvinists of her time, a Freudian might argue that this possibility is all the more significant. Extreme Calvinism could then be seen as contributing to mass hysteria, mass paranoia, or some other sort of mass psychosis. A Freudian might argue that the kind of deep conviction of personal evil revealed in this poem could easily be projected onto others, in, perhaps, accusations of witchcraft or other ungodly behavior. A Freudian might conceivably find in this poem evidence not so much of a particular personal mental illness as of a larger social irrationality.

FEMINIST critics might be deeply troubled by this poem. If we assume that the speaker of this poem is in fact female, the poem might especially disturb a feminist. After all, the speaker abases (and perhaps even debases) herself before a powerful male. She fears him and is terrified by the severe punishment he may inflict on her. A feminist might even argue that she reacts to this most powerful male in her life as a victim of abuse might react to a terrifying father or husband. She does not even dare look at him (1); she fears his angry face (2); she is confused and weeps (3); and she falls to her knees and cannot even stand up before him (5). She begs for his mercy (6), she sighs and groans (7–8), and she fears his dreadful wrath (11). She fears being expelled from his presence (12–13), and finally she hopes he will forgive her if she promises to repent (14). Many abused women, in Locke's day as well as in our own, could and can readily identify with these emotions and with this conduct.

But what if the speaker is not in fact a female? What if the speaker is imagined, instead, as simply any generic Christian? In that case, a feminist might still argue that the speaker is *being treated* as if the speaker were a woman and *is responding* in the ways many women have responded to physical and/or mental abuse. The speaker, in other words, occupies the "subject position" of a woman even if the speaker is not in fact female. To the extent that the speaker feels weak, helpless, and inferior in the face of overwhelming male power, the speaker is in a common position occupied by many women in Locke's era and in our own.

ECOCRITICS might have relatively little to say about this poem and the many other Renaissance poems it resembles. That fact alone, however, is significant. Locke's sonnet, like much literature of her period, has almost nothing at all to say about the natural environment. Environmental concerns are missing from this poem as they are missing from much writing of Locke's era. This fact is not very surprising. People of Locke's time had less reason to worry about the ultimate fate of the environment than do people living today. When Locke was living, the world was still a place of natural abundance. Even if an environmental crisis (such as "global warming" or "climate change") had been looming, people in Locke's era would have had few if any ways of suspecting it or detecting it. And, of course, they had not yet developed the kinds of "weapons of mass destruction" (whether atomic or biological) that might raise the possibility of destroying all, or nearly all, life on earth. Thus, the relative lack of concern with "environmental issues" in Renaissance literature can actually be seen as implying the environment's relative health during that era.

Yet that lack of concern can also (as this poem clearly suggests) indicate a very fundamental indifference to *this* world—this present, physical, natural environment. Lock's speaker seems much less interested in life on earth than in life in either heaven or hell. The existence that truly mattered to Lock and her speaker was the existence to come—an existence in which the natural environment of this world would play no part at all.

HAVE MERCY, GOD, FOR THY GREAT MERCY'S SAKE

Haue mercie   Have mercy, God, for thy great mercy's sake.
vpon me (o   O God: my God, unto my shame I say,
God) after thy   Beinge fled from thee, so as I dread to take
great merci   Thy name in wretched mouth, and fear to pray
   Or ask the mercy that I have abused.   [5]
   But, God of mercy, let me come to thee:
   Not for justice, that justly am accused:
   Which self word Justice so amazeth me,
   That scarce I dare thy mercy sound again.
   But mercy, Lord, yet suffer me to crave.   [10]
   Mercy is thine: Let me not cry in vain,
   Thy great mercy for my great fault to have.
   Have mercy, God, pity my penitence
   With greater mercy than my great offense.

LONGINUS might admire this poem for its moral and spiritual seriousness. The speaker (the Biblical David from the scriptural psalms) is holding himself to extremely high and exacting moral and spiritual standards. He shows almost no interest in material desires or possessions. Instead, what matters most to him is the state of his soul and his relationship with God. Longinus would respect this speaker for all these reasons. Yet the poem cannot be called "inspiring" in any simple, usual sense of that word. It does not show the speaker feeling ecstatic, elevated, or exulted. Nor does the poem arguably have a particularly uplifting impact on readers. Its tone is excited and impassioned (traits Longinus might appreciate), but many readers might (and do) find this work depressing. Ultimately, however, one's reaction to this sonnet probably depends on one's fundamental religious assumptions. To the extent that the poem implies the glory, power, and mercy of God, it might appeal to Longinus and especially to readers who value the majesty of God more than their own emotions.

THEMATIC critics might emphasize the poem's key word and key theme: "mercy." That term is used ten times in fourteen lines. Mercy is a crucial concept that helps shape our experience not only of this poem but of Locke's entire sequence. The contrast between mercy and justice is reiterated frequently both in this sonnet and in many that follow. The poem encourages us to think about the nature of mercy and justice as well as about the nature of God and humans. To the extent that we respond to this poem by pondering the ideas it deals with, we are responding as thematic critics. Merely by repeating the word "mercy" so often, the poem's speaker never lets us lose sight of the work's "central theme" or leading "motif." It is as if the speaker turns the idea of mercy over and over again in his mind, considering it from many different angles, and thereby encourages us to do the same. Note, too, the way the speaker juxtaposes the idea of mercy with opposing ideas that help define it and help make us appreciate mercy's enormous importance. Thus, mercy is juxtaposed with justice in lines 7–8, and later "They great mercy" is paired with "my great fault" (12), while God's "greater mercy" is set over and against the speaker's "great offense." Few works so emphatically deal with single ideas as Lock deals with the idea of mercy in this particular sonnet.

ARCHETYPAL critics might be especially intrigued by this poem. After all, this sonnet might seem of interest to Christians only, and perhaps even only to Calvinist Christians. Why should a non-Christian (or someone not affiliated with, or even interested in, Judeo-Christian traditions), consider this poem worth reading? Why and how (more importantly) should such readers find the poem powerful or moving? Why and how might an atheist, for instance, be stirred by this sonnet? Archetypal critics would respond to all these questions by suggesting that this text, if it is powerful at all, is powerful partly because it plays on basic elements of human nature. One needn't be a Christian or Jew, for instance, to feel the sense of having offended a powerful superior, or of having fallen short of meeting exacting expectations. One needn't be religious to feel overwhelming guilt and a deep desire for forgiveness. Atheists, agnostics, and people of all attitudes about religion (or no attitudes about religion at all) do feel, have felt, and probably always will feel the kinds of emotions this poem expresses and exploits. These emotions include (in addition to the ones already mentioned) shame, desperation, fear, amazement, and a yearning for pity. Emotions like the ones this poem explores and voices are probably rooted in one of the most basic, inevitable, and universal of all human relationships: the relationship between parents (especially father) and child. The fear of having offended one's father or mother has probably existed everywhere and always and is unlikely ever to disappear from human nature.

STRUCTURALIST critics are interested in the ways people impose order on reality by seeing it in terms of mutually defining "binaries," or opposites. These binaries fit together in self-reinforcing codes or structures that help organize our thinking, perceptions, and experiences. In this poem, for instance, various binaries are present. They help structure the poem and also reflect larger ideological structures that exist outside the poem. Thus, the basic binary that helps structure this poem is the distinction between humans (on the one hand) and God (on the other). Humans are creatures; God is the creator. Humans deserve justice, but God can grant mercy. Humans should feel deep shame, whereas God personifies righteousness. Humans are insignificant but God is great. Powerless humans should feel fear when faced with God's infinite power. Humans are wretched, while God is glorious. Humans need to appeal to God, and God is the object of their appeals. Humans, in short, are fundamentally flawed because they are sinful, whereas God is absolutely perfect because of his righteousness. A structuralist would claim that all these binaries are crucial to the structure of Lock's poem, and that they also reflect one of the most basic, most pervasive codes of her culture at large: the Christian code that structured so much else in her life and the lives of her contemporaries.

DECONSTRUCTIVE critics seek to show how apparently simple codes are actually full of irresolvable contradictions. Deconstructors think that seemingly clear opposites contaminate or bleed into one another, so that nothing is ever as simple as it might seem to structuralists and other thinkers for whom reality seems relatively easy to make sense of. To begin the process of deconstruction, deconstructors will typically first show how apparently neutral, objective opposites actually involve a hierarchy, in which one term is "privileged" over the other. In the case of Lock's poem and the habits of mind it epitomizes, the terms that are privileged are relatively obvious. Thus, God is privileged over humans, the creator is privileged over his creatures, glory is privileged over wretchedness, and so on. God seems to be the firm, stable center, whereas humans are associated with instability and mutability. Deconstructors might note, however, that definitions of "God" have been anything but stable in human history. Numerous kinds of gods have been imagined throughout time, and Lock herself was living during an era when Christians were killing each other over different, conflicting ideas about God. Similarly, deconstructors might suggest that whereas

God in Lock's poem is considered the source of both justice and mercy, it is possible to argue that God is neither just nor merciful. One need only mention the infamous "problem of evil" to make this point: if god is just, how and why does he permit the innocent (such as small children) to suffer? If he is merciful, how (again) does he allow unmerited pain to exist? If God is perfect, how and why does he seem to behave in such imperfect ways? If humans can rationally judge God's moral imperfections, who is more powerful, the so-called creator or his so-called creatures? If God is immutable, why have there been so many different gods throughout human history?

The point of deconstruction is not to establish a new set of hierarchies or privileged terms but to show how unstable and liable to interpretation and reinterpretation all hierarchies and privileged terms are likely to be if examined closely. In Locke's poem, even such an apparently simple term as "my God" (2) can be subject to opposite interpretations. On the one hand, the phrase can imply that God has complete power and authority over the speaker and defines the speaker's entire existence. On the other hand, the phrase can be "deconstructed" and be read as revealing that the speaker's "God" is indeed merely that: the speaker's own *personal interpretation* of God. After all (a deconstructor might claim), the inability to agree about definitions of God has been one of the most persistent of all human inconsistencies.

4

Sir Philip Sidney (1554–86):

Astrophil and Stella 5 ("It is most true"); *Astrophil and Stella* 71 ("Who will in fairest book")

Despite his exceptionally premature death from a wound received in combat, Sir Philip Sidney left behind one of the most influential legacies of any writer of the English Renaissance. His literary achievements seem all the more impressive when we realize that for Sidney creative writing was a hobby rather than a profession. He wrote in his spare time, not to make money but to articulate ideas that were important to him. He also, of course, hoped to enhance his reputation as a learned man during a time when learning had become an increasingly important trait for aristocrats at the court of Queen Elizabeth I (1533–1603), who was herself an unusually learned monarch.

Sidney wrote (besides much else) the *Arcadia*, one of the longest and most important works of prose fiction in English history; the *Apology for Poetry*, one of the most influential defenses of literature ever composed; and *Astrophil and Stella*, the first Petrarchan sonnet sequence in English—a sequence that set off a craze for English sonnet-writing during the Elizabethan period. Devoutly Christian and devotedly Protestant, Sidney is widely thought to have used his writing to promote his religious ideas. Whether and how this may be true in *Astrophil and Stella*, however, remains up for discussion. In simplest terms, this collection of sonnets and longer poems tells the story of the romantic obsession of "Astrophil" ("star-lover") for the beautiful Stella ("star"). Some readers assume that the sequence reflects Sidney's own passion for a married woman named Penelope Rich. Other readers see the sequence as an allegorical mockery of foolish, misguided erotic desire that leads nowhere and results in Astrophil's frustration. For the latter sort of readers, the sequence seems meant to teach moral lessons by presenting the negative (if often very comic) example of Astrophil's misguided infatuation.

ASTROPHIL AND STELLA 5

It is most true, that eyes are formed to serve
The inward light; and that the heavenly part
Ought to be king, from whose rules who do swerve,
Rebels to Nature, strive for their own smart.
It is most true, what we call Cupid's dart,   [5]
An image is, which for ourselves we carve;
And, fools, adore in temple of our heart,
Till that good god make Church and churchman starve.
True, that true beauty virtue is indeed,
Whereof this beauty can be but a shade,   [10]
Which elements with mortal mixture breed;
True, that on earth we are but pilgrims made,
And should in soul up to our country move;
True; and yet true, that I must Stella love.

PLATO distrusted most literature because he believed that it appealed to (and stimulated) irrational emotions. He believed that humans should be ruled by reason and logic. Literature, which almost by definition dealt with fiction, could therefore promote dangerous irrationality. If nothing else, it might be a waste of time. Poets and other writers (Plato believed) had little real knowledge of the subjects they wrote about; typically, they were experts in almost none of the topics they discussed. The only literature Plato was willing to permit in his ideal Republic was literature that confirmed (and made it easier for most people to understand) philosophical truth.

For all these reasons, Platonic critics might be suspicious of Sidney's *Astrophil and Stella*, which deals with a man's passionate desire for a woman. Platonic critics would want to know whether Sidney's poems endorse that desire or satirize it. Even satire and irony might be risky, since some readers might miss the joke and respond sympathetically (or even with empathy) to the lover's passions. In fact, one can make the case that this is precisely what has happened to Sidney's poems and others like them. Some readers have found Astrophil an immensely appealing figure, have enjoyed his pursuit of Stella, and have assumed that Sidney himself identified with Astrophil and that he sanctions Astrophil's passions.

A Platonic critic might note that in Sonnet 5 Astrophil, until the poem's very last line, seems to acknowledge many different kinds of religious, philosophical, and moral truths that were widely accepted in his day. Thus, in lines 1–2 he acknowledges the standard Christian "truth" that the senses were formed by God to serve the reason or soul. Likewise, in lines 2–3 he acknowledges the standard Christian belief that the mind or rational soul ought to rule human conduct. Similarly, in lines 4–5 he concedes that people who swerve from the rules of reason rebel against nature (i.e., against the reasons they were created) and therefore ironically strive to cause themselves pain. Lines 5–7 suggest that people who follow Cupid (i.e., pursue selfish desires) are idolators who foolishly replace the love of God with love of self. Line 8 acknowledges the standard assumption of Sidney's day that selfish desire could damage both the body (the "church") and the soul ("the churchman"). Lines 9–10 acknowledge the standard idea (derived from Plato, by the way) that intangible virtue is more beautiful than any physical thing and that anything truly beautiful is merely a shadow or reflection of virtue (and ultimately of God, the source of all virtue and of all real beauty). In line 11 Astrophil acknowledges that physically beautiful objects (such as other people) lose their beauty because that beauty is mixed with mortal, mutable elements (such as flesh) that inevitably decay. And, finally, lines 12–13 acknowledge the standard Renaissance belief that God created humans as "pilgrims" who were intended to seek their spiritual way back to him and their homeland of heaven.

Having spent thirteen lines admitting that he knows these standard Christian "truths" and that he acknowledges them to *be* true, Astrophil in line 14 nevertheless declares his continued "love" for Stella—a "love" which, he concedes, violates all the truths he has just accepted. In short, Astrophil's "love" is clearly irrational. Plato might note that the poem pretty obviously reveals and implicitly rebukes that irrationality. But Plato might wish that Sidney, in rebuking Astrophil, had relied less on irony and more on open, unambiguous statement.

FORMALIST critics, on the other hand, might admire the very irony that Plato might conceivably fault. Formalists believe that the best literature implies and suggests meanings rather than baldly and blandly stating them. The best writers (formalists believe) show rather than tell, because subtlety requires more skill than open statement. Formalists might argue that the irony at the end of Sidney's poem is hard to mistake and that the final ironic twist adds to the poem's witty closing impact.

But a formalist would find much more to admire about this poem than merely its ending. For example, the repetition of the phrase "It is most true" and the word "true" gives the poem a tight structure, effective rhythm, and emphatic focus on a central, unifying idea. Furthermore, the poem is full of memorable phrasing. Sidney uses concrete words, images, and metaphors to convey abstract ideas. Thus, reason is described as "The inward light" (2), and the soul is "the heavenly part" that should function as the "king" that rules over every other part of a human being. Line 6 subtly alludes to the biblical commandment against idolatry. Line 8 uses sarcasm when referring to Cupid as a "good" god, while the rest of that line uses metaphors to describe the body and the soul. Line 9 almost certainly puns on the word "indeed" (meaning both "truly" and "in action"). Lines 12–13 use an effective extended metaphor, so that moving "up to our country" (heaven) picks up on the earlier description of humans as "pilgrims"; and then, of course, line 14—with its heavily accented monosyllabic words—cleverly kicks the ladder out from under the whole rest of the poem.

A formalist might have much more to say about the nitty-gritty details of the poem (formalists always do), but this should be enough to suggest why they would admire the work so much as a work of *art*.

MARXIST critics, with their emphasis on improving material conditions for poor people on earth (in the here and now), might consider Sidney's poem a typical piece of religious propaganda. The poem takes for granted the existence of God, heaven, the soul, and the importance of living a life that conforms to standard Christian teachings. Marxists, on the other hand, would question or even deny all supernatural assumptions. For Marxists, religion is merely a means of distracting people from the worldly things that really matter. These include safe shelter, sufficient food, and freedom from poverty and servitude. Astrophil's only concern is Astrophil. His obsession with Stella prevents him from thinking about anyone besides himself. Rather than trying to improve practical living conditions for the people around him (especially those of lower socioeconomic standing than himself), he focuses obsessively on satisfying his own erotic desires. Marxists might agree with Plato that Astrophil is an irrational egotist, but Marxists might also argue that belief in a mythical God and in an equally mythical heaven provides no real solution to the practical social problems created by the self-centeredness of people like Astrophil.

DIALOGICAL critics, who are interested in the ways one text can allude to (or be "in dialogue with") other texts, might find Sidney's poem particularly fascinating. Clearly the poem alludes to the whole tradition of Christian texts as well as to the whole tradition of Petrarchan love poetry, with its heavy emphasis on the cruelty of Cupid. More specifically, Sidney's poem is "in dialogue with" commandments three and four of the Hebrew/Christian "ten commandments": (3) "Thou shalt have no other gods before me" and (4) "Thou shalt not make unto thee any graven image." Lines 5–8 of Sidney's poem allude to both commandments, just as they also allude to 1 Cor. 6:19 from the Christian scriptures: "know ye not that your body is the temple of the Holy Ghost *which is* in you, which ye have of God, and ye are not your own?" Line 10 alludes to the "allegory of the cave" from Book VII of Plato's *Republic*. It also alludes, more generally, to Plato's theory of "forms." According to this theory, everything on earth is merely a mutable, imperfect imitation of an abstract "form" or "idea." Thus, any single chair in which any human has ever sat is merely an imitation of the idea of "chair" or the concept of "chairness." In order to make the physical chair, one must first have access to the concept "chair." All the ideas just mentioned as present in Sidney's sonnet, like all the other ideas discussed in this poem, were exceptionally well known in Sidney's era. His sonnet is "in dialogue with" all of them, and the sudden switch from the rational religious voice of the first thirteen lines to the impassioned, irrational voice of the final line would also interest dialogical critics.

POSTMODERN critics might enjoy the switch from seriousness to playfulness in the final line. Sidney, in *Astrophil and Stella*, composed some of the funniest sonnets in the whole Petrarchan tradition. By constantly letting Astrophil reveal his own foolishness, Sidney combines what seems to be a serious moral intent with a comic presentation. Such mixing of tones might appeal to postmodernists. At the same time, postmodernists would almost certainly be suspicious of the "grand narratives"—the all-encompassing assumptions—on which this poem is built. For the first thirteen lines, Astrophil rattles off the common classical/ Christian beliefs that were the dominant ideas of his period and that sought to explain the nature and purposes of human life. Postmodernists are highly skeptical of any such attempts to make perfect sense of things, and so they might even applaud the final line of the sonnet. In that line, Astrophil impulsively throws overboard all the grand "truths" he has just acknowledged. Apparently he thinks that his own personal "truth"—his need for Stella—is more important than any of them.

ASTROPHIL AND STELLA 71

Who will in fairest book of nature know
How virtue may best lodg'd in beauty be,
Let him but learn of love to read in thee,
Stella, those fair lines which true goodness show.
There shall he find all vices' overthrow,   [5]
Not by rude force, but sweetest sovereignty
Of reason, from whose light those night-birds fly;
That inward sun in thine eyes shineth so.
And, not content to be perfection's heir
Thyself, dost strive all minds that way to move,   [10]
Who mark in thee what is in thee most fair.
So while thy beauty draws thy heart to love,
As fast thy virtue bends that love to good:
But "Ah," Desire still cries, "Give me some food!"

ARISTOTLE might find much to interest him in Sidney's sonnet, including such philosophical assumptions as the following: (a) the idea that nature can reveal meaning; (b) the objective existence of virtue and vice; and (c) the crucial importance of reason. Yet Aristotle would be interested not merely in the content of the poem (the ideas it expresses) but in its craftsmanship. He might, for instance, particularly admire the ways Sidney meets the demands of the sonnet genre (as in his skillful use of the Petrarchan rhyme scheme). Aristotle might also admire the way Sidney shows both his ability to write in perfect iambic pentameter meter (as in the first line) as well as his skill in altering that meter to emphasize key words, as in the first word ("Stella") of line 4. Indeed, Sidney often in this poem emphasizes the first syllables of his lines, just as he also skillfully uses alliteration (as in all the "l" sounds of line 3). He shows a sure command of metaphor (especially in line 7), a command that Aristotle considered one of the best indications of a true poet. Aristotle would, in short, admire any detail of this poem that revealed Sidney's talent as a craftsman. These details might include (for instance) the clever combination of alliteration and assonance in line 10, the balanced phrasing of line 11, and, especially, the abrupt but perfectly appropriate shift and outburst in the final line. Aristotle might conclude that only a truly talented artist could write a poem as rich and coherent as this example of the sonnet genre.

THEMATIC critics might be especially intrigued by the poem's emphasis on such obvious themes as virtue, vice, beauty, reason, the divine, perfection, and the ability of beauty to move the mind toward God. All these themes were quite important to much Renaissance literature, and so Sidney's sonnet might be seen as reflecting ideas significant not only to Sidney himself but also to his whole historical era. The poem might also interest a thematic critic because it is structured (until the final line) as a rational, logical argument. The purpose of the poem seems to be to remind readers of standard Renaissance Christian "truths" by using the skill and beauty of the poem to move readers toward a greater appreciation of reason and God. In this sense, then, the poem functions much as the speaker claims Stella does. But in the final line, of course, Desire disrupts the carefully wrought argument of the thirteen preceding lines. Thematic critics might suggest that this poem therefore illustrates once more a major theme of the entire sonnet sequence:

the conflict between passion and reason, between selfish interests and one's serious obligations to morality and God.

READER-RESPONSE critics are more interested in the actual responses of actual readers than in how readers might or "should" respond to a literary text. In particular, these critics are interested in the responses of readers either as individuals or as groups. For example, readers of Sidney's day might have responded differently to this sonnet than readers of other eras. Thus, sixteenth-century readers might have been shocked (but also amused) by the blatantly physical appetite expressed in the final line. For these readers (or at least many of them), that line might have been seen as an ironic confirmation of the Christian views the rest of the poem expresses. From this point of view, Desire's outburst merely confirms the fundamental selfishness Astrophil has been displaying all along. In contrast, readers of a more "Romantic" frame of mind might find the final line unfortunately crude. That line might threaten any tendency to see Astrophil as a lover ideally devoted to true love for the beautiful Stella. One guesses (although it would be interesting to know for sure) that this sonnet was *not* a favorite poem by Sidney among high-minded, genteel readers of, say, the Romantic or Victorian periods. On the other hand, it is easy to imagine many readers of the late-twentieth or early-twenty-first centuries, with their often hard-edged, unromantic, and even cynical points of view, enjoying the refreshing outburst of honest, undisguised lust that appears in the final line. And, finally, it is very easy to imagine different individuals from any period having specifically individual or idiosyncratic reactions to the poem based on their own personal attitudes or experiences. Imagine, for instance, how a rape victim might react to the final line.

NEW HISTORICIST critics might be especially interested in the power struggles implied in this sonnet. Thus, virtue is in conflict with evil; reason is in conflict with any vice that results from uncontrolled passion; and, in the final line, naked desire is in conflict with all the forces (including virtue and reason) that try to restrain it. In a sense, this poem might be seen by new historicists as one small reflection of the larger culture that produced it. All the conflicts the poem describes were also evident in the larger cultural system. Christian clerics, for instance, saw themselves as guardians of virtue and as obligated to control, suppress, or punish anyone or anything they regarded as vicious or immoral. Schools, universities, and other centers of learning had been established (often by Christians) to promote the disciplined development of reason and to oppose ignorance and mere emotionalism. Yet conflicts among Christians themselves in this period (even, or especially, among learned, educated Christians) made achieving unity and reaching agreement nearly impossible. Christians themselves often fought and even killed one another. Sir Philip Sidney himself, after all, died in a religious war. When complete suppression of opposing viewpoints proved impossible during the Renaissance, negotiations might be necessary. The outburst at the end of Sidney's sonnet suggests how difficult it is to entirely control, eliminate, or suppress opposition. This sonnet, in short, can be read as confirming the new historicist assumption that cultures are sites of conflict and negotiation.

DARWINIAN critics, who regard male sexual desire as a crucial, driving impulse behind all human life, would not be at all surprised by the outburst in the final line of Sidney's poem. Indeed, that line compares sexual desire to physical hunger, another very fundamental instinct that Darwinians consider innate (and in fact essentially irresistible) in all humans and indeed in all animals. Sidney's entire sonnet sequence can be seen in Darwinian terms: humans, who have highly evolved capacities to reason, often use reason to try to control self-destructive emotions. Their ability to reason at such an advanced level helps set them apart from the so-called lower animals. Reason allows humans much greater capacity for forethought and for control of their environments. It gives them an evolutionary advantage over other creatures—creatures lacking strong rational capacities. Little wonder, then, that so many of Sidney's poems can be read as reflecting the efforts of reason to control passion. Little wonder, too, that cultures throughout the world have developed methods for promoting such control. Doing so (it might be argued) has given (and still gives) such cultures distinct evolutionary advantages.

5

Edmund Spenser (1552–99):

Amoretti 68 ("Most glorious Lord of life"); *Amoretti* 75 ("One day I wrote her name"); *The Faerie Queene*, I.i-ii

AMORETTI 68

Most glorious Lord of life, that on this day
Didst make thy triumph over death and sin:
And having harrow'd hell, didst bring away
Captivity thence captive, us to win:
This joyous day, dear Lord, with joy begin,   [5]
And grant that we for whom thou diddest die,
Being with thy dear blood clean wash'd from sin,
May live forever in felicity.
And that thy love we, weighing worthily,
May likewise love thee for the same again: [10]
And for thy sake, that all like dear didst buy,
With love may one another entertain.

So let us love, dear love, like as we ought,
Love is the lesson which the Lord us taught.

Edmund Spenser was one of the many Elizabethan poets who admired and imitated the example of Sir Philip Sidney. Like Sidney, Spenser was a committed Protestant who used his poetry to comment on religious and political issues. Also like Sidney, Spenser wrote in a wide variety of genres. His *Amoretti* (or "Little Loves") resembles Sidney's *Astrophil and Stella* in being one of the very first English sonnet sequences. Meanwhile, his poem *The Faerie Queene* resembles Sidney's prose work, *The Arcadia*, in being long, romantic, epic in intent, and ultimately incomplete.

Spenser's *Amoretti*, like most Petrarchan sonnet sequences, tells the story of a male lover's desire for a beautiful woman. Unlike most other such sequences, however, Spenser's has a happy ending. The lover eventually learns to love the soul and character (not just the physical beauty) of the woman he desires. Realizing that he loves her truly, she loves him in turn, and the relationship ends in a sanctified Christian marriage.

HORACE, the classical Roman poet whose poems and ideas about poetry were so influential during the Renaissance, would have many reasons to admire *Amoretti* 68. Horace believed that poets should, first and foremost, write in ways that would appeal to their actual audiences. Spenser's poem would have appealed to many sixteenth-century readers in numerous ways. It is both Christian and romantic, endorsing love between a man and woman that reflects the love between humans and God. Moreover, the poem says nothing that would offend any readers of Spenser's day: Protestants, Catholics, and Christians of all sorts would be likely to find the poem appealing. Both women and men might enjoy this work, and even Christians otherwise suspicious of poetry would find nothing objectionable here. Yet this sonnet satisfies many other Horatian criteria: it is clearly written; its structure is lucid; it is a highly accomplished example of the sonnet genre; it both pleases and instructs; and it is traditional both generically and in the message it conveys.

TRADITIONAL HISTORICAL critics would be interested in the historical circumstances of this poem and in how those circumstances might be relevant to interpreting the work. For instance, *Amoretti* 68 was written during a time of immense and often bloody conflict between Protestants and Catholics, but this sonnet seems anything but sectarian. All Christians would probably agree with its theology and admire its tone. During a time when Christians often felt murderous rage for one another, this poem celebrates simple, all-pervasive love. Unlike some of Spenser's other poetry (which is sometimes militantly Protestant and virulently anti-Catholic), this poem's tone and message are both quiet and peaceful. Traditional historical critics would also almost certainly provide biographical information relevant to this sonnet. For instance, Spenser uses the *Amoretti* to celebrate his own love for Elizabeth Boyle, the woman he married in 1594, shortly before he published his sonnet sequence. Historical critics would want to know as much as possible about Boyle and about her relationship with Spenser. Meanwhile, Spenser's *Epithalamion*, the poem that immediately follows *Amoretti* in the first printing, is by definition a "marriage poem." Traditional historical critics might discuss the long history of such poems and might note that Spenser uses the genre in highly innovative ways: rather than celebrating the marriage of another couple, he celebrates his own. Knowing the history of prior epithalamia helps us appreciate the unusual traits of Spenser's own "marriage poem."

PSYCHOANALYTIC critics assume that the human psyche is often highly conflicted. The subconscious, emotional id (the seat of desires and fears) often rebels against the rational, responsible ego. It therefore needs to be supervised and controlled both by the ego and by the moral, ethical superego (which is often associated with the conscience or even God). In *Amoretti* 68, all conflict seems to have been eliminated. Perfect harmony seems to prevail. The poem begins by referring to God, the personification of the superego. Lines 9–10 encourage the rational ego to weigh (or properly evaluate and appreciate) God's love for humans so that humans may, in response, love God as he loves them. Finally, lines 13–14 show the speaker using reason to encourage a kind of love between him and his beloved that will be both profoundly rational and deeply spiritual. The irrational, selfish id is almost completely absent from this poem. The only pleasure the speaker endorses is pleasure consistent with reason and morality.

ARCHETYPAL critics assume that human beings are fundamentally the same in spite of superficial differences of culture, history, ethnicity, race, etc. Spenser's poem might therefore seem to present a real challenge to these critics. His sonnet might seem so rooted in a specific religion and historical era that it would have little appeal to readers of other times, places, and faiths. Archetypal critics might argue, however, that the poem actually draws on many fundamentally human desires and fears. One of these is the general desire to please authority figures, especially if those figures have sacrificed on one's behalf. The "Lord" here is also a loving father and, in the person of the crucified Christ, becomes a kind of selfless elder brother. The poem thus plays on a basic human impulse to be grateful to one's parents and to love one's siblings. Likewise, the poem is arguably rooted in a deep human desire for true love of another person and for lasting peace with one's fellow humans. An archetypal critic might contend that one need not be a Christian to appreciate the thoughts and emotions Spenser's poem reflects and expresses.

DIALOGICAL critics are interested in all the various ways texts can involve dialogue, either between the text and its audiences, between the text and other texts, between characters within the text, or in all these ways at once. Such critics are also interested in the different kinds of "voices" or tones a text might exhibit and in the interactions between them. Spenser's poem is largely structured by different kinds of address. It opens by addressing God (1–8), implicitly shifts to addressing other humans as well (9–12), and then finally ends by addressing the speaker's beloved (13–14). The first eight lines are almost a prayer; the next four are almost a sermon; while the final two seem lovingly intimate. Of course, in addressing God and his beloved, the speaker also always addresses his readers, and many of his lines echo not only the Bible but also many standard Christian texts (such as the Apostles' Creed). Dialogical critics might consider this a particularly rich poem in the number and nature of the voices it uses.

AMORETTI 75

One day I wrote her name upon the strand,
But came the waves and washed it away:
Again I wrote it with a second hand,
But came the tide, and made my pains his prey.
"Vain man," said she, "that dost in vain assay,   [5]

A mortal thing so to immortalize;
For I myself shall like to this decay,
And eke my name be wiped out likewise."
"Not so," (quod I) "let baser things devise
To die in dust, but you shall live by fame: [10]|
My verse your vertues rare shall eternize,
And in the heavens write your glorious name:
Where whenas death shall all the world subdue,
Our love shall live, and later life renew."

LONGINUS is the ancient Greek critic famous for his view that poetry should spring from and create in the reader a sense of lofty moral and spiritual elevation (or "the sublime"). The effect of the sublime, Longinus believed, is irresistible. Confronted with anything truly noble and inspiring, we are transported out of and above ourselves in a kind of ecstasy. Longinus might therefore admire Spenser's sonnet for numerous reasons. First, the poem reveals a noble sense of humility on the part of the speaker's beloved. The mere fact that she considers herself simply a "mortal thing" (6), doomed to be forgotten, shows an admirable lack of pride. That trait alone suggests her nobility of mind and soul. Responding to the lady's modesty, the speaker promises to "immortalize" her in his poetry: his works will "eternize" her "vertues rare" (6, 11). He intends to write poetry about her that will be so powerful, so effective and affecting, that their love will be remembered until the end of time. Then, during the Last Judgment, Christ (the most sublime of all figures imaginable) will literally raise them from the dead and give them the kind of elevation that surpasses anything that seems sublime in any mere earthly sense.

FORMALIST critics would find much to admire in this poem because they find much to admire in practically any well-constructed work of art. They might, for instance, praise the effective repetition in lines 1–4; the switch from narration to quoted speech in line 5; the wordplay in lines 5 and 6; the switch from monologue to dialogue in line 9; the alliterative use of "d" sounds in line 10; the alliteration and wordplay in line 11; the alliterative use of "w" sounds in line 13; and the extremely heavy alliteration of "l" sounds in the final line. This, however, is just the tip of the proverbial iceberg. Thus, formalists would admire the use of regular iambic pentameter meter in the poem's first four lines; the effectively emphatic violation of that meter in the first two syllables of line 5; and the return to iambic pentameter in the rest of the poem, so that the phrase "Vain man" (5) receives especially strong stress. Formalists might also enjoy the poem's memorable use of imagery (especially in lines 1–4 and 10), as well as its complex combination of tones, particularly as it moves from the mocking tone of line 5 to the lofty, almost prophetic tone of lines 11–14.

MARXIST critics might consider this a somewhat frivolous poem for several reasons. First, it deals entirely with a merely private relationship between two people. It reveals little concern for the practical welfare of others. It therefore exemplifies the kind of narcissistic self-focus typical of noncommunist societies. Second, the poem assumes, in its last three words, the Christian myth of resurrection and an afterlife. In fact, the entire poem is obsessed with personal immortality. This kind of obsession with a supposedly ideal future distracts people from the very practical business of making the present materially better for everyone. For all these reasons, a Marxist might consider the poem a typically superficial product of a typically self-centered, non-Marxist socioeconomic system.

FEMINIST critics might be truly intrigued by this sonnet. It is one of the relatively few love poems from the English Renaissance in which a woman is finally allowed to speak. Moreover, the voice of the woman we hear in this sonnet is strong, confident, appealingly modest, but even a bit cheeky. Rather than being overly concerned with (or proud of) her physical attractiveness, she considers it relatively unimportant. She does not seem especially bothered by the thought that her body will eventually "decay" (7). Apparently her body does not seem especially important to her. Moreover, the male speaker also seems less interested in the woman's body than in her character, her soul, her "vertues rare" (11). In short, this poem depicts the kind of relationship a feminist might admire—a relationship between an articulate, self-assured woman and a man who loves her for traits far more important than her good looks.

ECOCRITICS, concerned especially with humans' relationships with nature, might note that this poem begins by imagining the speaker on a beach near the ocean, writing his lady's name in the sand. The waves twice wash her name away, after which the speaker promises that he will write the lady's name "in the heavens" (12). Here, as in so many Renaissance poems, nature symbolizes mutability and inconstancy. Most Renaissance thinkers believed that anything made of atoms or the "four elements" inevitably decays. All earthly things—including human beings—are "mortal," as the lady herself acknowledges (6). In this sense, everything made of matter is "base" and will "die in dust" (9–10). Supernatural entities (such as the soul, spirit, God, and heaven) were considered superior, in the Renaissance, to anything that was part of merely material nature. This attitude (ecocritics might argue) can lead humans to ignore or devalue the physical environment. It can lead people to concentrate so much on the afterlife that they fail to be good stewards of nature while they live here on earth.

THE FAERIE QUEENE, I.i-ii

Spenser's *The Faerie Queene* is a long, complicated allegorical poem of epic scope and ambitions. It opens by describing a young knight riding on horseback.

i
A Gentle Knight was pricking on the plaine,
Y cladd in mightie armes and silver shielde,
Wherein old dints of deepe wounds did remaine,
The cruell markes of many a bloudy fielde;
Yet armes till that time did he never wield: [5]
His angry steede did chide his foming bitt,
As much disdayning to the curbe to yield:
Full jolly knight he seemd, and faire did sitt,
As one for knightly giusts and fierce encounters fitt.

ii
But on his brest a bloudie Crosse he bore,   [10]
The deare remembrance of his dying Lord,
For whose sweete sake that glorious badge he wore,
And dead as living ever him ador'd:
Upon his shield the like was also scor'd,
For soveraine hope, which in his helpe he had: [15]
Right faithfull true he was in deede and word,
But of his cheere did seeme too solemne sad;
Yet nothing did he dread, but ever was ydrad.

HORACE, the great classical Roman poet, was chiefly concerned that writers should please their audiences and not make fools of themselves. He advised poets to follow custom, because custom provided actual proof of audience interests and tastes. He might therefore admire Spenser for choosing to write a poem full of knights, damsels, monsters, and adventurous deeds. These topics had proven their popularity in previous European and English literature, as in the many different legends about King Arthur. By writing about such topics, Spenser was almost sure to appeal to many readers. Moreover, by choosing a deliberately archaic style, Spenser might also attract the many readers in England who admired the Arthurian legends as well as the many who considered Chaucer the greatest of English poets. Finally, by making *The Faerie Queene* so obviously didactic, Spenser was appealing to readers interested in poetry that would teach valuable moral and spiritual lessons while doing so in entertaining, interesting ways.

STRUCTURALIST critics are interested in the various codes humans use to structure reality. Normally these codes are rooted in "binary opposites" in which one term helps define the others. These stanzas, for instance, are structured by such explicit or implied opposites as the following: strength/weakness; spiritual/physical; experience/inexperience; maturity/immaturity; Christian/non- or anti-Christian. All the terms to the left of the slash marks are positive; all the terms to the right are negative. All the similar terms reinforce one another and contribute to the larger structure of the mindset that undergirds this poem. In addition, Spenser also relies in this work on various other codes with which his audience would have been familiar. These include the codes of Arthurian legend; the codes of Christian culture; the codes of medieval English; the codes of medieval romantic epics; and so on. Only by knowing all these codes could readers successfully interpret Spenser's poem. Knowing the codes is more important than knowing any particular manifestation of the codes. In other words, it is more important to study the codes than simply to interpret any particular text. By writing an extended allegory, such as *The Faerie Queene*, Spenser constructed an especially code-driven work, one in which particular meanings could easily be inferred by knowing the larger code. Thus, anyone familiar with the codes Spenser is employing here will realize almost immediately that the Knight is a representative Christian, that his appearance suggests his involvement in spiritual conflicts, and that the "dying Lord" (11) to whom he bears allegiance is Jesus Christ.

DECONSTRUCTIVE critics tend to find literary texts (and indeed all texts) much more messy, ambiguous, and even self-contradictory than structuralists do. Structuralists look for neat, orderly patterns; deconstructors try to show how nothing is ever really neat or orderly. In these opening stanzas of *The Faerie Queene*, for instance, Spenser—a deeply Protestant writer—uses Arthurian imagery that had long been associated with Roman Catholicism. Thus, although the knight who appears here seems at first to represent Christianity in general, later he will represent Protestantism in particular. Similarly, the opening stanzas already begin to suggest the importance of spiritual strength, spiritual heroism, and spiritual combat. But in the sixteenth century, of course, the Catholic and Protestant Christians who were killing each other were in fact often relying on brute physical strength to try to impose their views on one another. The battles implied in these opening stanzas, then, were not merely allegorical but quite literal. Nor were the actual battles quite as heroic as these stanzas might imply. Sometimes they involved vicious massacres of innocent civilians. Christians were killing each other precisely because they could not agree about interpretations, especially interpretations of the Bible. Deconstructors assume that all texts can be endlessly interpreted. In the sixteenth century as so often later, the "Word"— (or scripture, which literally means "writing")—was as open to different, irresolvable, contradictory interpretations as any other text. This fact would surprise deconstructors not one bit.

READER-RESPONSE critics, like deconstructors, essentially believe that there is no reason to expect that all readers will arrive at the very same interpretation of any text. For deconstructors, interpretative disagreements are generated by inconsistencies or contradictions in the texts themselves. For reader-response critics, disagreements are the results of the different assumptions, values, beliefs, and responses of different readers. Thus, although Spenser begins *The Faerie Queene* by presenting a knight who might seem at first to be a generic Christian, eventually the knight will be presented as a Protestant hero, doing battle with evil Catholicism. When this meaning becomes clear, it is safe to assume that Protestants and Catholics would (and will) respond to the poem very differently. The words on the page are the same for both kinds of readers;

what differ are the hearts and minds of the readers themselves. That difference (a reader-response critic would argue) makes *all* the difference in how the poem will be interpreted and received. Similarly, modern readers who dislike (say) archaic English or allegorical poetry might dislike Spenser's poem almost immediately, while those interested (say) in Arthurian legends and tales of heroic adventures might find this poem instantly appealing.

MULTICULTURAL critics, like reader-response critics, assume that responses to a text may vary widely depending on the identity of the reader. However, while reader-response critics tend in general to emphasize differences between different *individual* readers, multicultural critics tend to emphasize distinctions between different *groups* of readers. As noted above, Catholic readers might respond differently to Spenser's poem than Protestant readers. Irish readers might scoff at Spenser's supposed commitment to Christian virtue in light of his support for oppression of sixteenth-century Irish Catholics. Women readers might be suspicious of yet another poem in which a male character is the obvious hero (but might appreciate the fact that Spenser, later in the poem, does indeed present heroic women). It is even possible to imagine that some animal lovers might dislike the imagery here of an animal forced, by pain, to do the bidding of a human. And non- or anti-Christian readers might find the whole premise of the poem absurd or at least uninteresting. Reactions to a text depend, for multicultural critics, very much on the make-up of the subgroups reacting.

6

Christopher Marlowe (1564–93):

"The Passionate Shepherd to His Love"; "Hero and Leander" (excerpt)

"THE PASSIONATE SHEPHERD TO HIS LOVE"

Come live with me and be my love,
And we will all the pleasures prove
That valleys, groves, hills, and fields,
Woods, or steepy mountain yields.

And we will sit upon the rocks,   [5]
Seeing the shepherds feed their flocks,
By shallow rivers to whose falls
Melodious birds sing madrigals.

And I will make thee beds of roses
And a thousand fragrant posies,   [10]

A cap of flowers, and a kirtle
Embroidered all with leaves of myrtle;

A gown made of the finest wool
Which from our pretty lambs we pull;
Fair lined slippers for the cold,   [15]
With buckles of the purest gold;

A belt of straw and ivy buds,
With coral clasps and amber studs:
And if these pleasures may thee move,
Come live with me, and be my love.   [20]

The shepherds' swains shall dance and sing
For thy delight each May morning:
If these delights thy mind may move,
Then live with me and be my love.

"The Passionate Shepherd to His Love" is one of the most famous of all poems from the English Renaissance. It is a seduction poem, in which a shepherd tries to persuade a woman to love him and live with him. Marlowe's poem provoked various imitations and poetic responses by other major poets, including a notable poem written by Sir Walter Ralegh in which the woman responds to (and essentially rejects) the shepherd's appeals.

ARISTOTLE, the great literary theorist of ancient Greece, was primarily concerned with the genres of tragedy and epic in his famous work *The Poetics*. Nevertheless, general principles about poetry in the broadest sense can be deduced from his work. He was very interested, for instance, in matters of genre. He believed that poets wrote not simply "poems" in any general sense but different *kinds* of poems. Marlowe's text, for instance, is a lyric poem in the pastoral style. Aristotle believed that once a poet had chosen the kind of poem he wanted to write, he was obligated to make every detail of the poem consistent with the selected genre. The poem's "plot," characters, thought, and diction, for instance, should all be appropriate to the chosen genre.

Certainly Marlowe fulfills all of Aristotle's expectations. His poem is, in fact, one of the most influential pastoral lyrics ever written, precisely because it satisfies, and helps affirm, the expectations most people have of that genre. The "plot" of the poem is one of seduction or courtship (a very common plot in pastoral poetry). The poem's main "character"—its speaker—is an articulate, whimsical shepherd. His thoughts are thoughts of love and desire. And his diction is the kind of "middle" diction appropriate to such a poem: it is neither high-flown nor common, neither grandiloquent nor crude or slangy. All the details and imagery the poem mentions are appropriate to the *kind* of poem this is. Nothing seems surprising or out of place. This work exhibits the kind of coherence Aristotle expected of well-crafted literature.

FEMINIST critics—or at least some of them—might see Marlowe's poem as just one of many literary works in which women are the passive objects of male attention. Indeed, Ralegh's response to this poem—"The Nymph's Reply to the Shepherd"—is especially interesting not only because the speaker is a woman but also because she generally rejects the shepherd's pleas. In Marlowe's poem, as in so many other Renaissance "love" poems, only the male speaks; only the male's desires seem important enough to articulate. Some feminists might note that Marlowe's speaker tries to win the woman with gifts or bribes; he assumes that she can be "bought" with promises of material possessions (9–20). In particular, he assumes that promises of attractive clothing will win her—as if women are mainly interested in physical presents that will make them seem even more appealing to men. Some feminists might argue that the speaker assumes that the woman's mind and motives are somewhat shallow. The shepherd, after all, does not praise her character or her intellect. Instead, he offers her trinkets and clothes. Finally, he assumes that his male friends will help him win and maintain the woman's affection by dancing and singing for her—pastimes that may suggest her sensual and even sexual interests.

Alternatively, other feminists might suggest that the silent woman in this poem is in a position of relative power at this point in the couple's relationship. The man, after all, is courting *her* and seems almost desperate to please her. The poem ends with the woman having provided no response. Perhaps the balance of power in their relationship would have changed if she had given in to the shepherd's appeals, but, as the poem ends, she is still arguably in control, not only of herself but also of her suitor.

READER-RESPONSE critics focus on the ways real readers actually respond to literary texts. Rather than assuming that there is some ideal "correct" response, they note that real readers tend to respond in various different ways to anything they read. For a reader-response critic, the responses already suggested above are just three of many possible ways in which this poem might be reasonably interpreted and reacted to. Numerous other potential responses are easy to imagine. A young man, for instance, might sympathize with the young male speaker this poem presents. A young woman might find the young male speaker either appealing or annoying. Plato, or anyone else with a very serious disposition, might consider this poem, and poems like it, unappealingly frivolous. A deeply religious person might be bothered by the shepherd's emphasis on material gifts. An older person, long past the days of courtship himself or herself, might be amused by this poem's whimsical treatment of youthful romance. In short, the poem might provoke almost any number of plausible responses from almost any number of easily imaginable readers.

ECOCRITICS, who emphasize the interactions of humans and physical nature, might be interested not only in this particular poem but in the pastoral genre in general. After all, pastoral writings, almost by definition, emphasize shepherds, shepherdesses, and/or other people who live close to the land and who interact closely with sheep and/or other animals. Shepherds are people who cannot afford to ignore or exploit nature; they must care both for their animals and for the landscape they and the animals inhabit. Significantly, shepherds do not usually kill the sheep they raise; the sheep are more valuable alive than dead.

Marlowe's poem is appealing partly because it so memorably evokes the pleasures of a pastoral landscape (2–4). Humans, plants, animals, birds, rivers, and even rocks are closely involved with one another (5–8). There is no sense of either literal or metaphorical distance between humans and nature. Indeed, their connection is so close that the speaker imagines clothing for humans being made of wool, flowers, and even leaves (11–18). Nature in this poem seems abundant both in beauty and in the useful goods it can provide. Ecocritics might value poems of this sort because they help encourage love of nature and appreciation of the natural environment.

DARWINIAN critics might emphasize how closely the "plot" of this poem conforms to Darwinian ideas about relations between the sexes. In this poem, as in much of nature, a male must do everything possible to win the attention and cooperation of a female. The male must do the courting; he is the one who must compete to be successful; and the female is the one who is in control of the relationship at this point (although perhaps not later). The poem imagines courtship in a rural environment, not in a city, and indeed rural environments would have been the place where most courtship rituals would have occurred for most of the history of the human race, and even before humans in the strict sense came into existence. The male speaker performs to win the woman's cooperation; he promises to give her things and might, for that very reason, be attractive to her. After all, Darwinians suggest that whereas males mainly tend to seek as many sexual partners as possible, human females have a vested interest in finding males who will provide for them, make a commitment to them, and help nurture any children who result from a sexual relationship. Darwinian critics, then, would find this poem almost a textbook illustration of the typical roles of men and women in human relationships.

"HERO AND LEANDER" (EXCERPT)

"Hero and Leander" is a fairly lengthy, unfinished "epyllion," a kind of narrative poem much longer than a lyric but much shorter than an epic. Such poems became especially popular in the late sixteenth century. Marlowe's poem was one of the most famous and influential. Like Shakespeare's "Venus and Adonis," it deals with the erotic relationship between a handsome young man (Leander) and a beautiful female (Hero).

> Amorous Leander, beautiful and young
> (Whose tragedy divine Musæus sung),
> Dwelt at Abydos; since him dwelt there none
> For whom succeeding times make greater moan.
> His dangling tresses, that were never shorn,   [55]
> Had they been cut, and unto Colchos borne,
> Would have allur'd the vent'rous youth of Greece
> To hazard more than for the golden fleece.
> Fair Cynthia wish'd his arms might be her sphere;
> Grief makes her pale, because she moves not there.   [60]
> His body was as straight as Circe's wand;
> Jove might have sipt out nectar from his hand.

Even as delicious meat is to the taste,
So was his neck in touching, and surpast
The white of Pelops' shoulder: I could tell ye,   [65]
How smooth his breast was, and how white his belly;
And whose immortal fingers did imprint
That heavenly path with many a curious dint
That runs along his back; but my rude pen
Can hardly blazon forth the loves of men,   [70]
Much less of powerful gods: let it suffice
That my slack Muse sings of Leander's eyes;
Those orient cheeks and lips, exceeding his
That leapt into the water for a kiss
Of his own shadow, and, despising many,   [75]
Died ere he could enjoy the love of any.
Had wild Hippolytus Leander seen,
Enamour'd of his beauty had he been.
His presence made the rudest peasant melt,
That in the vast uplandish country dwelt;   [80]
The barbarous Thracian soldier, mov'd with nought,
Was mov'd with him, and for his favour sought.
Some swore he was a maid in man's attire,
For in his looks were all that men desire,—
A pleasant smiling cheek, a speaking eye,   [85]
A brow for love to banquet royally;
And such as knew he was a man, would say,
"Leander, thou art made for amorous play;
Why art thou not in love, and lov'd of all?
Though thou be fair, yet be not thine own thrall."   [90]

PLATO believed that literature, if it were allowed to exist at all, should help promote morality, reason, and selfless devotion to the good of society. He disdained excessive interest in anything material, mutable, emotional, and superficial. He would therefore be immediately suspicious of the poem's emphasis on Leander's beauty and youth (51). Both are impermanent and appeal only to crude emotions. Nothing in this description says anything about Leander's character or virtue; instead, merely sensual attractions are emphasized (and the same is true of the immediately preceding description of Hero). Poetry of this sort (Plato believed) made the Greek gods look lustful and therefore ridiculous, and some

Christians of Marlowe's own day would probably also have seen this kind of poetry as too worldly, too sexual, and too shallow to be worth writing or reading.

STRUCTURALIST critics, who emphasize the ways cultural codes are rooted in mutually reinforcing binary opposites, might look for the underlying code(s) embedded in this passage. Thus, the reference to beauty (51) implies its opposite: ugliness. The reference to youth (51) likewise implies the contrary (old age). Youth and beauty are mentioned together because they are part of the same overarching structure—a structure greatly defined by opposites. Similar reinforcing opposites continue to appear and continue to suggest an important underlying structure of the poem. Such opposites include the following (with the implied term inside square brackets): long hair/[baldness] (55); youthful adventure/[the timidity of the old] (57); bravery/[fear] (58); sensual pleasure /[lack of pleasure, or even disgust] (62–3); smooth white skin/[wrinkled, discolored skin] (65–6). This list could easily be extended, but by now the point is clear: Marlowe's description reflects a culture that prized youth, good looks, strength, bravery, sensual pleasure, smooth sensual skin, and the vitality implied by long hair. By the same token, that culture disdained decrepit old age, physical ugliness, timidity, fear, anything disgusting, and the decay in appearance caused by aging. A few lines from Marlowe's poem, therefore, suggest a great deal about the culture that produced him and his writing. Knowing the underlying codes he echoes and reinforces can help us better understand not only this poem but also Elizabethan culture in general.

DECONSTRUCTIVE critics look for the gaps, contradictions, and irresolvable paradoxes that they believe can be found in any text and any cultural code. Thus, the distinction between beauty and ugliness cannot be maintained, if only because beauty almost always fades with time (at least in living things, and even in many nonliving things). Beauty is valued so much precisely *because* it is impermanent and mutable. The same is true, of course, of youth: we value youth precisely because we know it will not last. Thus the apparently clear distinction between youth and age collapses. Practically every other distinction mentioned above (in the discussion of structuralism) similarly collapses: the strength of youth gives way to the weakness of old age; the bravery of youth gives way to the timidity of old age; smooth skin becomes wrinkled with time; and the luxuriant hair of youth often becomes gray, retreats, or disappears entirely. All the neat distinctions postulated by structuralists, therefore, seem radically unstable to deconstructors, and they can seem unstable in multiple ways. For example, the implied distinction between youthful strength and the weakness of old age is undercut whenever we find a young person who is weaker than someone much older. Nothing, for the deconstructors, is ever as simple and clear-cut as it tends to seem to structuralists and advocates of other, more traditional ways of thinking. Even Leander, the handsome young man, is described in ways that make him sound almost stereotypically feminine in appearance, with his long hair, his smooth, white skin, and his ability to attract the erotic attention of both males and females simultaneously.

MULTICULTURAL critics, who emphasize the importance of minority populations within any culture, would be especially fascinated by this passage from Marlowe's poem. Leander's good looks are described in ways that undermine or at least complicate traditional ideas about gender. Marlowe, who probably had homosexual desires himself, certainly seems here to create a passage remarkable for its time in its emphasis on youthful male beauty. (A passage near the end of the poem, in which Leander swims naked, is even more surprising.) Multicultural critics might suggest that the quoted passage would have appealed to anyone with homoerotic feelings in Marlowe's era, and that the passage can still excite similar interests today. Especially interesting is the suggestion that Jove, the male king of the gods, would find Leander sexually attractive (although Jove was famously bisexual in his interest in humans). But Leander stimulates the erotic interest of many other males, including unsophisticated peasants and barbarous soldiers (79–82). One need not be a figure of classical myth, in other words, to find Leander sexually alluring. Multicultural critics might argue that passages such as this provide firm historical evidence for the existence of same-sex desire in Marlowe's day. They might also suggest that such passages suggest that same-sex desire has always existed and will always exist, no matter how strenuously different cultures may sometimes seek to suppress it. The acts of reading and valuing such passages (multiculturalists might say) help open our eyes and minds to the existence of an important minority culture that deserves recognition, toleration, and respect. No culture, they would argue, is really monolithic; all cultures are, almost by definition, multicultural.

POSTMODERNIST critics are skeptical of any grand narratives and totalizing explanations. They doubt efforts to achieve neat, tidy, self-consistent understandings of cultural phenomena. Those phenomena (they think) are likely to be extremely complicated, if not chaotic. In this sense, postmodernists have much in common with deconstructors. For all these reasons, postmodernists might be inclined to emphasize the *bi*-sexual, transsexual, transgender, and/or transvestite implications of the quoted passage. Leander provokes desire as much in women as in men, and his good looks are almost conventionally feminine (73–4; 84–6). To some observers, he almost looks like a woman dressed in male clothing (83). He excites the erotic interest of practically everyone, including gods, goddesses, human males, human females, peasants, soldiers, and just about anyone else who sees him. His very existence calls into question any system rooted in rigid ideas about gender. He does not, for instance, fit easily into the ideas about male and female roles and motives propounded by recent Darwinian critics. Darwinians tend to emphasize that males are interested in females, and vice versa. Leander, however seems, by his very nature(s) and by the multiple desires he arouses in many different kinds of people and deities, to undermine any simple ideas about sexuality. Postmodernists would not be at all threatened by this fact but would instead celebrate it. And they would also see it as evidence for their basic assumption that "grand narratives" that try to offer simplistic explanations should be greeted with great skepticism.

7

William Shakespeare (1564–1616):

Sonnets 3 and 147; "Venus and Adonis" (excerpt)

SONNET 3

Look in thy glass and tell the face thou viewest,
Now is the time that face should form another,
Whose fresh repair if now thou not renewest,
Thou dost beguile the world, unbless some mother.
For where is she so fair whose uneared womb   [5]
Disdains the tillage of thy husbandry?
Or who is he so fond will be the tomb
Of his self-love, to stop posterity?
Thou art thy mother's glass, and she in thee
Calls back the lovely April of her prime;   [10]
So thou through windows of thine age shalt see,
Despite of wrinkles, this thy golden time.
But if thou live rememb'red not to be,
Die single and thine image dies with thee.

Shakespeare's *Sonnets* reflect the immense interest in the sonnet form in the late sixteenth century. Earlier sonnets (such as those by Wyatt, Surrey, Sidney, and Spenser) were strongly influenced by Petrarch. Petrarchan sonnets usually depict a man obsessed with a beautiful, virtuous woman. Shakespeare's sonnets, however, differ from this pattern in two major respects. First, many are addressed to a handsome young man, whom the older speaker encourages to marry, settle down, and have children. Second, the woman who finally does appear in the late sonnets is a woman of ill repute, often called "the dark lady." Shakespeare, then, exemplifies a very common practice in Renaissance poetry: he uses a common genre, but he writes in ways that give that genre his own distinctive stamp.

ARISTOTLE valued carefully constructed literature—literature that demonstrated the writer's skill and that appealed to an innate human instinct for organic unity. Every part of a good text (he believed) should be appropriate to every other part and should contribute to a complexly unified design. For these reasons, Aristotle would probably admire this sonnet (and probably all of Shakespeare's sonnets). In this poem, the speaker encourages the handsome young man to cheat death by having children, presumably after marrying. By having children, the young man will be able to see his own youth reflected in them as he ages, just as his mother can presently see her youth reflected in him.

The poem is unified by the consistency of its arguments, yet it achieves complexity by the varied ways those arguments are restated. At first, the argument is offered as straightforward advice (1–4). Then, in lines 5–8, the argument next takes the form of two rhetorical questions relying on brief analogies. In lines 9–12, the argument is reiterated again, but this time through an extended analogy. Finally, after this lengthy statement (9–12), the poem concludes very abruptly and emphatically by offering an ironic choice.

As the poem develops, Shakespeare demonstrates many of the skills Aristotle expected of a well-crafted work, including (among much else), memorable metaphors, especially in lines 5–6. Aristotle believed that the ability to create metaphors—to perceive unity others might overlook—implied poetic genius. Rather than being an acquired skill, it was a rare mental gift.

THEMATIC critics emphasize the ways literature reflects and expresses key *ideas*, also known as "themes" or "motifs." Thematic critics (unlike Aristotle, and more like Plato) are less interested in *how* a text is written than in *what* it "says" (or implies). They look for the ways themes *do* help unify works, but they also tend to be interested in ideas in and of themselves. They assume that we read literature even more for the ideas it deals with than for the skill with which it is written.

The central theme of Sonnet 3 (and of many of Shakespeare's other sonnets, and of much Renaissance literature in general) is arguably the theme of mutability. This is the idea that almost everything earthly constantly changes and deteriorates. Mutability is often associated with decay that leads to death. It is a chief concern of Shakespeare's writings, and thwarting mutability was the main goal of many of his contemporaries. One way to defeat mutability was to believe in God and hope for eternal life. Another way (as Shakespeare will suggest later in the sonnets) is to write—or be the focus of—great literature. Finally, the method emphasized in Sonnet 3 is having children. Producing children is a way both to create positive change and to ensure continuity. All the various implied and explicit references in Shakespeare's poem to mutability indicate his (and his readers') desire to cheat (and defeat) death.

ARCHETYPAL critics (like Aristotle and most other ancient theorists) believe that great literature springs from, and appeals to, elements of a widespread and tenacious human nature. They think the greatest literature is rooted in our most innate and most widely shared fears and desires, as well as in other very common experiences and psychological traits. Shakespeare's sonnet, for example, arguably appeals to such very basic human yearnings as our desires to be remembered, to combat aging, to produce children, and (above all) to overcome death. An archetypal critic might argue that one reason for the conflict the poem suggests is an opposition between two very basic human instincts: on the one hand, the youthful desire for freedom, and (on the other hand) the desire to live on, in some way, into the future.

DIALOGICAL critics are interested in all the various kinds of interaction—of give-and-take—that literary works can depict, imply, or engage in. In this sonnet, for instance, the unidentified speaker immediately addresses the handsome young man, but the opening lines may also imply an even wider audience. After all, many humans are interested in the subject of having children, and many are even more interested in cheating death. Yet dialogical critics might note that Shakespeare's speaker not only addresses the young man but literally asks him questions (5–8). By the time we reach lines 9–12, the speaker seems to have a specific addressee particularly in mind. Now, in a sense, he is addressing the young man not only as a representative young person but also as a particular youth whose mother is still living. Finally, in the closing couplet, the focus seems to widen again: the poem's last two lines seem addressed as much to readers in general as to any single reader in particular. But the poem is not only in dialogue with its readers but also with other texts. This is especially true since the poem is part of a sonnet *sequence*: each sonnet builds on the one before it and prepares for the one that follows. The first fifteen or so of Shakespeare's sonnets all make basically the same argument (have children to defeat death), and so Sonnet 3 is part of a developing dialogue involving the speaker, the young man, other readers, and other poems in the sequence. The poem uses different kinds of speech (arguments, declarations, questions)—a variety of methods and tones that would also interest dialogical critics.

DARWINIAN critics would suggest that this poem deals with the most fundamental of all evolutionary concerns: the need to reproduce in order to pass on one's genes (a bit of oneself) to the next generation. This poem emphasizes reproduction in the strictly literal sense: the passing on of one's actual physical appearance. In later sonnets, the speaker will also emphasize being preserved as part of a cultural legacy. Cultural evolution occurs when distinct "memes," or bits of information, are passed from one generation the next, either individually (as, say, a famous proverb) or collectively (as, say a memorable and remembered sonnet or sonnet sequence).

Darwinians would say that this poem is rooted in very fundamental biological issues. Presumably the young man likes sex. In fact, presumably he is all too willing to have it (which, a Darwinian would say, would be true of most males). The speaker, then, seems to be trying to persuade the young man to have *legitimate* children through sex within a legally recognized marriage. Marriage, according to many Darwinians, has mutual advantages for both men and women. First, it ideally assures each man and woman that his or her partner is sexually faithful. Second, it gives the woman confidence that a man will help her raise her children. Darwinians would be surprised by nothing at all in Shakespeare's sonnet.

SONNET 147

My love is as a fever, longing still
For that which longer nurseth the disease,
Feeding on that which doth preserve the ill,
The uncertain sickly appetite to please.
My reason, the physician to my love,　　　　　　　　　　[5]
Angry that his prescriptions are not kept,
Hath left me, and I desperate now approve
Desire is death, which physic did except.
Past cure I am, now reason is past care,
And frantic-mad with evermore unrest;　　　　　　　　　[10]
My thoughts and my discourse as madmen's are,
At random from the truth vainly express'd;
For I have sworn thee fair and thought thee bright,
Who art as black as hell, as dark as night.

In this sonnet, one of the darkest ever written, the speaker expresses self-disgust for having surrendered to lust. Specifically, he succumbed to sexual desire for the "dark lady," an attractive woman of dark complexion (and even darker character) who enters Shakespeare's sequence late in its development. Although the speaker realizes she is sexually promiscuous and unfaithful, he has had sex with her anyway (see, for instance, Sonnet 138). Sonnet 147, one of the last poems in the collection, expresses his self-revulsion but also condemns the woman herself.

PLATO could admire moral literature—that is, literature that helped people to distinguish right from wrong and encourage them to choose virtue over vice. He might therefore admire Sonnet 147 because it graphically emphasizes the dangers of uncontrolled passion. Lust is likened to sickness (1) and an addiction (2–3). Reason is compared to a doctor capable of curing lust, but only if his advice is followed (5–7). The speaker, having rejected reason, has now learned that lust is a kind of death, precisely as his reason had warned (7–8). Like any addiction, lust results from, and leads to, a surrender to unreasonable passions (9–12). The final two lines, addressed to the "dark lady," memorably summarize one aspect of the speaker's irrational behavior. Plato would probably value this poem because it implicitly endorses reason by attacking unrestrained passion.

TRADITIONAL HISTORICAL critics would show how an understanding of common Renaissance ideas could help us comprehend this sonnet's meaning. Such critics might argue, for instance, that the word "love" in this period could refer to two basic and contrasting ideas. The first, known as *caritas*, was love of God and love of anything or anyone as God would want us to love. The second, known as *cupiditas*, was selfish desire, rooted first and foremost in love of oneself. *Caritas* was true, virtuous love; *cupiditas* was not really love at all. Instead, it was selfish lust. Sonnet 147 arguably reveals the consequences of choosing *cupiditas* instead of *caritas*.

Another common Renaissance belief involved the opposition between reason and passion. Passion was often symbolized as a horse; reason was often symbolized as a rider. The rider was expected to keep the horse tightly reined in and under control. Shakespeare, instead of using this common analogy, instead likens reason to a doctor and the speaker to a rebellious patient. Yet the fundamental meaning is still the same: reasonable behavior is good; passionate conduct is self-destructive. A traditional historical critic would cite numerous texts written during and before the Renaissance that make this fundamental distinction.

FORMALIST critics would be less interested in this poem's "meaning" than in the skill and effectiveness with which it is written. They might note, for instance, the memorable simile of line 1, the irony of the word "nurseth" in line 2 (ironic because nursing is usually associated with a restoration to health), and the emphatic use of alliterated "s" sounds in line 4. Line 5 employs a striking metaphor, and lines 6–7 develop that metaphor into a kind of "conceit" (or extended metaphor). At the start of line 8, the speaker uses a memorably abrupt, three-word statement emphasized by alliterated "d" sounds. Line 9 is skillfully balanced, with the clever word-play of "Past cure" and "past care." Similar balance contributes to the effectiveness of lines 13–14, and the poem ends by emphasizing especially memorable final nouns ("hell" and "night"). Formalists would argue that what the poem "means" is far less important than the effectiveness of its phrasing.

PSYCHOANALYTIC critics might argue that passion or "sickly appetite" (4) results from an uncontrolled "id," the seat of irrational desire in Freudian psychology. The "reason" the poem emphasizes (5, 9) is the Renaissance equivalent to the Freudian idea of the "ego," which is associated with recognizing and acknowledging reality, but which is also, according to Christian thinking, one of God's greatest gifts to humans. God, of course, is comparable to the Freudian "superego," the seat of morality and conscience. Thus, although Shakespeare's poem was written long before Freud, much of its meaning and many of its terms make perfect sense from a Freudian point of view. To a Freudian, this poem depicts what can happen when the id escapes the control of the ego and the superego. Behavior rooted in the id is often self-destructive and often has unfortunate consequences for society in general.

NEW HISTORICIST critics, with their interest in power relations, might note that this poem reflects conflicts within the larger culture of Shakespeare's time. One of the most effective ways to win and retain power in the sixteenth century was to claim that one was reasonable, mature, and acting as God's agent. One of the most effective ways to deny power to others was to claim that they were irrational, immature, and ungodly. By using this poem to implicitly condemn irrational passion, Shakespeare aligns himself with the values most prized in his culture—values of reason, self-control, and morality. By making the speaker condemn the passion to which the speaker himself has succumbed, Shakespeare makes that condemnation far more powerful than if the speaker had merely preached a sonnet sermon. In the poem's final line, however, the speaker turns from expressing self-contempt to expressing deep disgust with the woman he seems to blame for tempting him. It is as if the speaker, even when confessing his own sins, cannot refrain from trying to preserve at least a bit of his power and self-respect by partly blaming the woman.

VENUS AND ADONIS

EVEN as the sun with purple-colour'd face
Had ta'en his last leave of the weeping morn,
Rose-cheek'd Adonis hied him to the chase;
Hunting he loved, but love he laugh'd to scorn;
Sick-thoughted Venus makes amain unto him,   [5]
And like a bold-faced suitor 'gins to woo him.

"Thrice-fairer than myself," thus she began,
The field's chief flower, sweet above compare,
Stain to all nymphs, more lovely than a man,

More white and red than doves or roses are;   [10]
Nature that made thee, with herself at strife,
Saith that the world hath ending with thy life.

"Vouchsafe, thou wonder, to alight thy steed,
And rein his proud head to the saddle-bow;
If thou wilt deign this favour, for thy meed   [15]
A thousand honey secrets shalt thou know:
Here come and sit, where never serpent hisses,
And being set, I'll smother thee with kisses . . ."

Venus and Adonis describes the pursuit of an extremely handsome young man (Adonis) by Venus, the goddess of love. This poem was one of the most popular of Shakespeare's works during his own lifetime. It is his version of an epyllion, the genre made most famous by Christopher Marlowe's *Hero and Leander* (see Chapter 6).

PLATO, who emphasized the need for literature to be moral and to promote virtue, would surely be disturbed by these lines. He and many of Shakespeare's own contemporaries might have assumed that the poem is either endorsing or at the very least failing to censure mere sensual desire. Even if it could be argued that the poem is ironic (that it is mocking Venus rather than presenting her sympathetically), Plato and readers like him might wonder why the poet did not condemn sensuality more explicitly and obviously. Irony (Plato might argue) can easily be either missed or misunderstood. The history of literature is full of examples of readers failing to perceive irony intended by authors. Therefore Plato and readers like him might wonder whether ironic writing is worth the risk the author runs of being misinterpreted.

TRADITIONAL HISTORICAL critics would probably try to situate *Venus and Adonis* in some definite historical context(s). Almost certainly they would examine other examples of epyllia, both from the classical period and from the Renaissance itself. They would try to determine whether Shakespeare echoes any previous examples of this genre. They would also explore any similarities and differences between his presentation of Venus and Adonis and the ways those figures are presented in other works. They might, for instance, consult the sources discussed in a work such as H. David Brumble's very valuable book *Classical Myths and Legends in the Middle Ages and Renaissance: A Dictionary of*

Allegorical Meanings. And they might also try to determine when and why Shakespeare wrote this poem and how it was received by its original readers.

FORMALIST critics would examine as many details as possible from this passage to try to determine why and how the passage is effective as a piece of *poetry* (rather than as a statement of ideas or a piece of historical evidence). They might, for instance, comment on the personification used in lines 1–2, the imagery used in lines 1–3 (and throughout), and the balance and reversal (known as *chiasmus*) evident in line 4. Formalists might comment on the use of the historical present tense in lines 5–6, suggesting how it adds to the lines' sense of immediacy, and they might also discuss the emphatic, effective use of listing in lines 7–10. Formalists would also want to determine the *tone* of this passage, especially since it is the opening passage of the entire text. How seriously (they would ask) should we take it? Is Shakespeare having fun with us and the characters? If so, what specific evidence in the passage supports this sort of interpretation?

PSYCHOANALYTIC critics would surely be interested in the various psychological dimensions of this passage. These dimensions might include what the passage suggests about (1) the characters depicted, (2) the audiences by whom the passage would have been read, (3) the speaker of the poem, and (4) the poem's author. Especially interesting, from a psychoanalytic point of view, is the reference to "Sick-thoughted Venus" (5). This phrase most obviously implies that Venus is "love-sick," but one wonders if the phrase has any deeper connotations and may already be suggesting an ironic perspective on the goddess's pursuit of Adonis. Also intriguing is the moment when she calls Adonis "'Thrice-fairer than myself'" (7). In using such phrasing, is she displaying pride or humility? Is she implying her own beauty (and thus saying that Adonis is even more beautiful than she is)? Or is she simply implying that he is so astonishingly good-looking that she feels relatively unattractive beside him? In any case, psychoanalytic critics would almost certainly comment on her strong sexual impulse, driven by her unconscious "id."

FEMINIST critics might be especially interested in this passage because it depicts a female taking the sexual initiative. Venus acts as a male would conventionally act in sixteenth-century society, whereas Adonis is put into the position faced by especially attractive women of that era. Venus is the pursuer; Adonis is the pursued;

and it is clear that her interest in him is mainly physical. Some feminists might sympathize with Venus's motives; others might find it intriguing that in this poem a man gets to experience how it feels to be courted incessantly. In either case, feminists would almost certainly find it interesting that stereotypical gender roles are being played with, and perhaps even seriously questioned, in a passage such as this.

8

John Donne (1572–1631):

"The Flea"; "Holy Sonnet 14"

THE FLEA

Mark but this flea, and mark in this,
How little that which thou deniest me is;
It sucked me first, and now sucks thee,
And in this flea our two bloods mingled be;
Thou know'st that this cannot be said   [5]
A sin, nor shame, nor loss of maidenhead,
   Yet this enjoys before it woo,
   And pampered swells with one blood made of two,
   And this, alas, is more than we would do.

Oh stay, three lives in one flea spare,   [10]
Where we almost, nay more than married are.
This flea is you and I, and this
Our marriage bed, and marriage temple is;
Though parents grudge, and you, w'are met,
And cloistered in these living walls of jet.   [15]
   Though use make you apt to kill me,
   Let not to that, self-murder added be,
   And sacrilege, three sins in killing three.

Cruel and sudden, hast thou since
Purpled thy nail, in blood of innocence?   [20]
Wherein could this flea guilty be,
Except in that drop which it sucked from thee?
Yet thou triumph'st, and say'st that thou
Find'st not thy self, nor me the weaker now;
'Tis true; then learn how false, fears be: [25]
Just so much honor, when thou yield'st to me,
Will waste, as this flea's death took life from thee.

HORACE, the great Roman writer whose poems and ideas about
poetry were so influential during the Renaissance, would probably
admire much about "The Flea." First, the speaker's character
remains consistent throughout the text, thus contributing to the
work's unity. Second, the language is simple, plain, straightforward,
and easy to comprehend (unlike the language in certain other
poems by Donne). There is nothing "difficult" about this work—a
fact that helps explain its popularity as a classroom text. Third, the
poem is capable of appealing to various kinds of readers, as anyone
who has ever taught it can testify. For those who like wit, it has
wit. For those who like humor, it has humor. For those who like
their wit and humor to raise serious moral issues, this poem does
that. For anyone with a taste for irony, this is a pleasurably ironic
poem. In many ways and on many different levels, it displays the
kind of craftsmanship Horace valued. Its structure, for instance, is
both lucid and well designed, with the speaker first acting (in stanza
one) as a desperate suitor, then (in stanza two) as a kind of defense
lawyer, pleading for the flea's life, and finally (in stanza three) as
a kind of prosecuting attorney, indicting the woman for abruptly
killing the insect. Whether one finds the speaker genuinely clever
or instead a fool who merely *thinks* he is clever, this poem is a
proven crowd-pleaser. Custom (the voice of generations of satisfied
readers) has given its sanction to this work. In writing "The Flea,"
Donne pleased many readers, and, for Horace, pleasing readers is a
writer's chief responsibility.

TRADITIONAL HISTORICAL critics might want to determine
how "original" a poem this is—that is, whether it is as unusual a
work as it seems to many modern readers or whether it was part
of a tradition of such poems. In fact, Donne's text reflects a long
heritage of texts about fleas, especially *poems* about fleas, including

an "Elegia de Pulice" (elegy concerning a flea) long (but falsely) attributed to the influential Roman poet Ovid. H. David Brumble, in an especially fascinating article about Donne's poem, has argued that both Donne and many of his readers would have been familiar with Renaissance flea lore and that their knowledge of flea legends and flea poetry would have contributed to an ironic reading of this particular poem. According to this argument, Donne presents the speaker mockingly, so that the wit of the poem depends on its very "use of tradition rather than in any disregard of tradition." The poem's speaker, Brumble asserts, "uses reason, perverse reason, for wrong ends" (Brumble 152–3). Whether or not one finds this argument persuasive (as I in fact do), it illustrates a typical use of traditional historical criticism: to provide relevant information about how an author and his contemporary audience might have understood the meaning of a work later readers might misinterpret because they lack such information.

FORMALIST critics would be interested in any particular detail of this poem that contributed to its artistic effectiveness. Every single word and even sound would matter to a formalist. Thus a formalist might note how the poem immediately plunges us into the midst of a literally dramatic situation in which two people are present but only one of them speaks. By opening with the word "Mark," the speaker begins with an emphatic, accented, monosyllabic verb, while the word "this" instantly contributes a sense of specificity, and then the repeated words "mark" and "this" not only add emphasis but also make the first line's structure seem carefully balanced. Line one catches us by surprise because it immediately violates the iambic rhythmic pattern we might have expected (in which odd syllables are unstressed but even syllables are stressed). But that expected pattern soon reasserts itself and is used throughout the rest of stanza one. Donne, in other words, clearly knows when, where, why, and how to vary the rhythms of his lines for maximum dramatic impact. It would be easy to move through the rest of the poem, word by word and line by line, and show how this text is carefully constructed and carefully phrased. Such craftsmanship would make a formalist admire Donne's talent as a poet.

DIALOGICAL critics are especially interested in the ways texts, authors, and/or characters in texts interact with audiences, other texts, and/or other characters. They might be particularly intrigued by the fact that "The Flea" presents a kind of dialogue between the male speaker (who does all the talking) and the female he is courting. She never actually speaks (we never hear her own unmediated voice), but it is she who determines the course of their interaction, first by refusing his overtures, then by threatening to crush the flea, and then by actually crushing it—all the while continuing to refuse the male's attentions. Indeed, at the very end of the poem she speaks indirectly, when the male reports that she "triumph'st, and say'st that thou / Find'st not thy self, nor me the weaker now" (23–4). But of course the male will not let her have the last word (or any actual word of her own at all): he feels compelled to have the final say. The poem thus ends as it began: with the male continuing his argument, relentless to the end. Anyone who wants to read the poem ironically (i.e., as mockery of the cocky male speaker) will thereby see another layer of potential dialogue in this work, as the author of the poem implicitly satirizes the male who only *seems* to control the whole text. If the poem is read ironically, the joke is on the speaker, as the author offers a knowing wink, to the poem's readers, about the speaker's foolishness.

DARWINIAN critics would be surprised by nothing in "The Flea." The male speaker, desperate to have sex with the woman and desperate to think of any possible way to convince her to have sex, acts in ways that Darwinians could easily have predicted. Apparently the male and female are not married, and apparently she is still a virgin (6). From a Darwinian point of view, she has very good reason to be quite choosy in selecting a sexual partner, especially in a period before effective birth control. Yet even if birth control were foolproof during Donne's era, the young woman still would want to be careful in choosing a partner, particularly if she wanted eventually to have children. It would be to her practical advantage to choose a mate who would be willing to invest the time, energy, and commitment to a serious marriage and help her raise her children for the many years that task would take. A male whose sexual appetite was so strong that he could not commit to a faithful, monogamous relationship would not make an especially reliable partner. The poem's speaker, like most males, has (according to Darwinians) an innate interest in impregnating as many women as possible, without necessarily feeling any need to commit to any single one of them. Donne's speaker, flea-infested though he is, still considers himself an appealing lover.

HOLY SONNET 14

Batter my heart, three-person'd God, for you
As yet but knock, breathe, shine, and seek to mend;
That I may rise and stand, o'erthrow me, and bend
Your force to break, blow, burn, and make me new.
I, like an usurp'd town to another due,   [5]
Labor to admit you, but oh, to no end;
Reason, your viceroy in me, me should defend,
But is captiv'd, and proves weak or untrue.
Yet dearly I love you, and would be lov'd fain,
But am betroth'd unto your enemy;   [10]
Divorce me, untie or break that knot again,
Take me to you, imprison me, for I,
Except you enthrall me, never shall be free,
Nor ever chaste, except you ravish me.

LONGINUS, an ancient Greek theorist who emphasized the importance of "sublimity" (or elevation), would probably find much to admire in Holy Sonnet 14. After all, Longinus believed that the most effective writing was ethical, ecstatic, passionate, ennobling, inspired, and inspiring. Donne's sonnet arguably displays all these traits. The speaker yearns fiercely for a complete spiritual transformation, and he expresses this yearning in language that is both excited and exciting, especially in the first four lines. For many readers, the effect of this poem is nearly irresistible, as Longinus believed great writing should be: "sublime" writing or speech should hit us with the impact of a lightning bolt, sweeping us off our feet rather than merely offering a careful, rational argument. It should seem intellectually, morally, and spiritually powerful, transforming us with the kind of force the sonnet's speaker here attributes to God. Yet great writing and speech should (Longinus thought) also display craftsmanship, art, and intelligence. Donne's sonnet displays all these characteristics, especially in such features as the powerful opening verb of line 1, the string of emphatic verbs in lines 2–4, the vivid simile of line 5, the emotional interjection of "oh" in line 6, and the extended metaphor of lines 7–8. Donne also displays his skill in using the Petrarchan sonnet form, taking a genre usually associated with secular love and employing it for passionate wooing of God. The final line, with its daring, almost sexual reference to being "ravish[ed]" by God, ends the poem on an especially surprising and emphatic note. Longinus would surely consider this poem "sublime" in all the best senses of that word: it expresses the speaker's yearning not just for moral improvement but for a complete spiritual renovation that will rescue and elevate him utterly.

MARXIST critics, with their deep suspicions of religion (which Marx called the "opiate of the masses"), might dislike this poem precisely *because* it is so passionate and potentially powerful. Instead of encouraging people to think rationally about religion (a Marxist might say), Donne's poem actually discourages rational thought. The same strings of emphatic verbs that other readers might admire as artistically effective (in lines 2–4) might strike a Marxist as evidence of either foolish or devious emotion. In other words, either the speaker himself is giving in to irrational impulses or he is deceitfully playing on the irrational impulses of his readers. Or perhaps he is doing some of both: perhaps the speaker really believes the nonsense (as a Marxist might see it) he is peddling. In any case, a Marxist might argue that the speaker reveals himself as a kind of masochist, more than willing to submit to authoritarian power. He almost seems to enjoy groveling before a God (a figment of the imaginations of powerful people, who use this nonexistent being to intimidate, control, and distract the powerless). He claims to value "Reason" (7), but there is little about this poem that would seem reasonable from a Marxist point of view. Persons like the speaker allow the powerful to flourish, not only because they fail to resist them but because they so readily submit to their own degradation. The poem's final images—which imply that the speaker is willing to be imprisoned, enslaved, and even raped by God—might profoundly dishearten some Marxists. Such language (they might say) suggests an actual pleasure in being abused and exploited.

FEMINIST critics—or at least some of them—might be disturbed by Donne's sonnet for many of the same reasons it might disturb some Marxists. In some ways the speaker resembles an abused woman who seeks further abuse and even welcomes being battered. Symbolically, the speaker occupies a feminine "subject position" in this poem. In other words, though presumably a male biologically, the speaker arguably behaves (and is treated) as if he is a woman. He has come to believe that the punishment he craves is "for his own good," and, rather than resisting it, he is all too willing to submit to it and even desire it. He has either convinced himself, or been brought up to believe, that the all-powerful male who controls his life has his own best interests at heart. The sexual connotations possibly present in lines 6 and 14 might especially interest feminist critics. In line 6, the speaker wants to be penetrated by God; in line 14 he wants to be metaphorically raped. The speaker is torn between two powerful males (Satan and God), and the possibility of true independence and genuine freedom never seems to occur to him. Feminists might argue that even though the poem never explicitly mentions a female, the phrasing and the mindset it reflects are quite relevant to the experiences of many women during Donne's day and in all the years before then and later.

READER-RESPONSE critics might argue that this poem reflects the fact that almost any work can provoke widely divergent reactions from different readers or different *kinds* of readers. Many Christian readers might find the poem immensely appealing, although some Christians might actually consider it overblown and even off-putting in the way it depicts the Christian god, particularly in the final line. Atheists might find the poem tedious, uninteresting, unfortunate, or even laughable. Agnostics might consider it an interesting but ultimately unpersuasive work, while any adherent of a faith opposed to the Christian faith might regard Donne's poem as potentially offensive and misleading. Some readers (like formalists) might argue that the paraphraseable "meaning" of the poem is almost beside the point, and that what really makes the poem worth reading is the skill with which it is written. In short, the number of possible reactions to this text or practically any other text is (from the perspective of a reader-response critic) nearly limitless, and there would be little point in arguing that one reaction is "superior" to another.

NEW HISTORICIST critics are especially interested in issues of power, particularly in the ways power relationships affect actual persons rather than abstract entities (such as nations or states). New historicists might argue, for instance, that Donne's sonnet reflects a whole array of power relationships in Donne's society, in which relations with authority figures were especially important. Most of those authority figures, in Donne's era, would have been males, beginning with God and then extending down through kings, archbishops, bishops, dukes, earls, priests, patrons, actual fathers, and older brothers, to mention just a few. For Catholics, that list would also have included popes in particular. Of course, Donne lived many of his younger years during a time when a woman (Elizabeth I) occupied a position of enormous authority, and he also had to deal with many other powerful women. Yet most of the powerful persons in his life, and the lives of his contemporaries, were men. And, whatever the gender of the powerful person, accommodating oneself to such persons was crucial.

In this sonnet, the speaker offers total submission to the most important authority figure of all. In a sense, of course, he has little choice, because God by definition is all-powerful, whether one chooses to admit it or not. Paradoxically, however, a case can be made that by humbling himself before God, the speaker actually attempts to enhance his own power. By confessing his own sins and foolishness, he rejects sinfulness and folly. By admitting his lack of reason, he reasserts his rationality. By acknowledging God's omnipotence, he attempts to win back some of the power he feels he has forfeited through disobedience and sin. He adopts a posture that must have been typical of many people in Donne's day (and indeed in any period or place of authoritarian rule): the posture of absolute humility was a posture most likely to be effective. Yet Donne's speaker expresses his humility in especially witty, clever, inventive ways. He wins our respect (except from anyone who would positively refuse to grant it, such as an atheist or Marxist) by playing the role of humble suitor with much talent, intelligence, and aplomb.

9

Aemilia Lanyer (1569–1645):

"Eve's Apology in Defense of Women" (excerpt); "The Description of Cookham" (excerpt)

From Eve's Apology in Defense of Women

Until fairly recently, the writings of Aemilia Lanyer (sometimes also spelled "Emilia Lanier") were almost totally ignored. However, Lanyer and her works have benefited from the intense interest during the last several decades in recovering and discussing the writings of Renaissance (or "early modern") women. Lanyer's collection of poems titled *Salve Deus Rex Judaeorum* (Hail, God, King of the Jews) contains the following section (excerpted here) in which the speaker defends Eve from the common charge that the very first woman deserves blame for all the suffering that resulted from the loss of paradise.

Our Mother Eve, who tasted of the Tree,	Eve's
Giving to *Adam* what she held most deare,	Apologie

Was simply good, and had no powre to see;   [765]
The after-comming harme did not appeare:
    The subtile Serpent that our Sex betraide,
    Before our fall so sure a plot had laide.

That undiscerning Ignorance perceav'd
No guile, or craft that was by him intended;   [770]
For, had she knowne of what we were bereavid,
To his request she had not condiscended
But she (poore soule) by cunning was deceav'd,
No hurt therein her harmelesse Heart intended:
    For she alleadg'd Gods word, which he denies,   [775]
    That they should die, but even as Gods, be wise.

But surely *Adam* can not be excus'd,
Her fault, though great, yet hee was most too blame;
What Weaknesse offerd, Strength might have refus'd,
Being Lord of all, the greater was his shame: [780]
Although the Serpents craft had her abus'd,
Gods holy word ought all his actions frame:
    For he was Lord and King of all the earth,
    Before poore *Eve* had either life or breath.

Who being fram'd by Gods eternall hand,   [785]
The perfect'st man that ever breath'd on earth;
And from Gods mouth receiv'd that strait command,
The breach whereof he knew was present death:
Yea having powre to rule both Sea and Land,
Yet with one Apple wonne to loose that breath,   [790]
    Which God hath breathed in his beauteous face,
    Bringing us all in danger and disgrace.

And then to lay the fault on Patience backe,
That we (poore women) must endure it all;
We know right well he did discretion lacke,   [795]
Beeing not perswaded thereunto at all;
If *Eve* did erre, it was for knowledge sake,
The fruit beeing faire perswaded him to fall:
    No subtill Serpents falshood did betray him,
    If he would eate it, who had powre to stay him?   [800]

HORACE, the ancient Roman writer whose poetry and ideas about literature had such a huge influence on Renaissance authors, might find much to admire about the passage quoted above. It satisfies many standard Horatian criteria. After all, Lanyer's subject (the fall) was of immense interest to most of her intended audience (Renaissance Christians). She writes about a traditional topic in a way that most of her readers would have found easily accessible. By offering a defense of Eve, she varies to some degree from usual treatments of the fall, but she does not vary in any really extreme or radical ways. (After all, she admits Eve's fault but merely says that Adam's blame was greater.) Her phrasing is simple and clear, and, by using predictable stanza structures, she imposes order on the poem and thus displays her poetic skill. By using the word "our" (763, 768, 778, etc.) the speaker makes common cause with all of the poem's readers, thus attempting to appeal to the widest possible audience. At the same time, the speaker also tries to appeal to women in particular, as in the reference to "our Sex" in line 777. Her phrasing, however, runs little risk of alienating male readers (almost all of whom would have freely admitted Adam's guilt). If Lanyer's lines had been perceived as overtly offensive, there is little chance that they would have been published in her era, or perhaps even written.

TRADITIONAL HISTORICAL CRITICS would probably seek to determine just how unusual Lanyer's lines might have seemed to readers of her own period. Such critics would examine as many documents of that time (and earlier) as possible, including not only poems but also theological treatises and any other texts that might reveal the ideas about Eve with which Lanyer and readers of her day would likely have been familiar. Only by possessing thorough, reliable knowledge about how the poem would have been interpreted in Lanyer's time (such critics would say) can we determine the meaning Lanyer probably intended and conveyed. Any evidence of actual reactions to the poem (in the form, say, of marginal annotations, letters, diary entries, allusions in other poems, etc.) would be especially helpful in helping us say how the poem was actually understood by its first readers. In addition, any evidence about Lanyer's intentions in writing these lines would indicate how the poem should probably be interpreted. Traditional historical critics would also help explain why the poem is punctuated as it is. Lanyer often uses commas where modern writers would use semicolons or periods, such as at the ends of lines 765, 773, 777, and 779. Historical critics would explain that the rules of punctuation have often differed from one era to another and even in different places at the same time. Partly for this reason, such critics either prepare modernized texts of Renaissance poems (to make such poems easier for modern readers to comprehend) or they instead insist on presenting texts faithful to the original manuscripts or printings (to preserve even the smallest details of the original punctuation, spelling, syntax, and other matters).

FEMINIST CRITICS would obviously be very interested in "Eve's Apology," and in fact it is largely thanks to the influence of feminist criticism that texts like this one have been so widely sought out, studied, and republished during the past fifty years. Feminists would argue that the neglect of such texts reflects the sexism that has dominated most cultures throughout history. Lanyer's poetry (they would contend) has been overlooked not because it is less worthy than the poetry of many male writers but simply because Lanyer was a woman. And the same is true, of course, of the works of many other women writers. But Lanyer's lines are interesting not only because they were written *by* a woman but because they were written *about* one of the most famous women of all. Eve has been blamed by many male writers for destroying the happiness that humans originally enjoyed during the first couple's existence in the Garden of Eden. In that sense, Eve would symbolize, for feminists, all the women who have ever been unfairly blamed for ruining the happiness of others, especially men.

Feminists might note how Lanyer's lines seem designed to appeal to women readers without altogether alienating males. Thus, when line 763 refers to "Our Mother Eve," the word "Our" probably includes men as well as women, but when line 767 refers to "our Sex," women are clearly the intended audience. Then, in the very next line, the speaker refers to "our fall" (768), thus including men again. Feminists might also be intrigued by the ways the speaker turns the tables on any men who believe males are intellectually superior to women. If they are (the speaker implies), then Adam should easily have been able to resist being tempted by Eve: "What Weaknesse offerd, Strength might have refus'd, / Being Lord of all, the greater was [Adam's] shame" (779–80). Lanyer's speaker co-opts many patriarchal assumptions about the differences between men and women and thereby lays the blame for the fall squarely on Adam's shoulders. As she bluntly puts it at the end of this passage, "If he would eate [the forbidden fruit], who had powre to stay [i.e., stop or prevent] him?" (800). Ultimately (the speaker suggests), it was Adam, not Eve, who bore (and bears) the responsibility for human sin and suffering.

STRUCTURALIST CRITICS would be interested in any and all of the "binary opposites" that help structure this passage. Binary opposites help to mutually define one another as (for instance) hot helps define cold and light helps define darkness. And, if hot and light are similar to one another, and cold and darkness are similar to one another, a larger structure of opposites begins to emerge. In "Eve's Apology," numerous binary opposites are readily evident. In the following list, for instance, each term to the left of a slash mark is the opposite of each term to the right: Mother/father; Eve/Adam; lacking power/possessing power; women/men; being betrayed/making a deliberate choice; being deceived/exercising free will; being ignorant/possessing knowledge; being weak/being strong; being poor/being lordly, etc. All the terms to the left of the slash marks are associated with Eve; all the terms to the right are associated with Adam. Taken all together, the opposites reflect the assumptions and thinking that underlie the entire passage.

DECONSTRUCTIVE CRITICS would examine many of the same "binaries" noted by structuralist critics, but deconstructors would do more than simply note them or show how they reinforce one another. First, deconstructors would show how each binary is not merely a neutral descriptive pairing but is actually an implied hierarchy. Thus, in Western culture, fathers have been presumed to be the superiors to mothers; Adam has been presumed to be Eve's superior; possessing power has been presumed to be superior to lacking power; men have been presumed to be superior to women; and so on.

Having once revealed the hierarchical nature of such pairings, deconstructors would then seek to show how these apparently neat distinctions are actually unstable and begin to collapse or bleed into one another. In a sense, the whole point of "Eve's Apology" is to deconstruct the traditional, patriarchal narrative of the fall—a narrative that emphasized Eve's responsibility. Lanyer's poem undermines this narrative, suggesting that although Adam was traditionally perceived as stronger, more intelligent, more powerful, and more knowledgeable than Eve, it was actually Adam, when he ate of the fruit, who behaved in ways that were weaker, less intelligent, and less rational than Eve's behavior. The effect of Lanyer's "Apology" is not to make Eve seem better, more intelligent, or more rational than Adam (since such an argument would only establish a new, if different, hierarchy). Rather, the effect of Lanyer's lines is to undermine and complicate hierarchical assumptions altogether.

From the Description of Cookham

Lanyer's "Description of Cookham," published in 1611 as part of *Salve Deus Rex Judaeorum*, is a lengthy work of over 200 lines. It celebrates an estate where Margaret Clifford, the Countess of Cumberland, sometimes resided. Lanyer herself stayed there in some capacity, and in the opening lines she thanks the countess for encouraging her to write.

Farewell (sweet Cooke-ham) where I first obtained
Grace from that grace where perfect grace remained;
And where the muses gave their full consent,
I should have power the virtuous to content;
Where princely palace willed me to indite,   [5]
The sacred story of the soul's delight.
Farewell (sweet place) where virtue then did rest,
And all delights did harbor in her breast;
Never shall my sad eyes again behold
Those pleasures which my thoughts did then unfold.   [10]
Yet you (great Lady) Mistress of that place,
From whose desires did spring this work of grace;
Vouchsafe to think upon those pleasures past,
As fleeting worldly joys that could not last,
Or, as dim shadows of celestial pleasures,   [15]
Which are desired above all earthly treasures . . .

LONGINUS, who emphasized "sublime" ideals, emotions, and language, would probably admire this poem's opening lines for the ways they emphasize such lofty, noble traits as grace (2), virtue

(4, 7), spirituality (6), and elevated, permanent pleasures (15) rather than lowly, earthly, and impermanent satisfactions (16). Longinus would probably also admire virtues the poem displays even when it does not explicitly mention them. These include gratitude (2), appreciation of true nobility (4), virtuous poetic power (4), and faith in noble ideals (6). The speaker's praise of noble values and persons implies her own nobility of character. Longinus believed that only a truly noble person could produce a truly sublime work of art. Yet the selected lines also reveal the poet's intelligence and skill, especially in such lines as line 2 (with its clever word-play); lines 1 and 7 (with their similar beginnings); and lines 15–16, with their balanced contrasting of "celestial pleasures" and "earthly treasures." Although addressed to the Countess of Cumberland in particular, these lines ideally appeal to the best motives and traits of all human beings. For this and for many other reasons, Longinus would almost certainly admire this opening passage of Lanyer's poem.

THEMATIC critics, who are especially concerned with the key ideas a text emphasizes, would probably be particularly interested in the ways these lines either reiterate or touch on a number of key motifs. These include grace (2, 12), art (3), virtue (4, 7), spirituality (6), and especially pleasure (6, 10, 13–16). The emphasis on pleasure is particularly intriguing. By recalling the past pleasure of others, the speaker here attempts to give her readers present pleasure, partly by remembering and re-creating the pleasures she has herself enjoyed. If one wanted to argue that pleasure is a "central theme" (or "key idea" or "leitmotif") of this passage, doing so would not be difficult. All the other themes already mentioned (grace, art, virtue, spirituality, etc.) can be seen as specific examples of the more general theme of pleasure. Thematic critics often operate in this fashion: they often look for broad themes that unify subsidiary ideas. Such themes help reveal the unity of the entire work and they also help suggest the writer's skill in creating and sustaining such unity. It would not be difficult, for instance, to imagine an essay on this passage (and perhaps on the whole poem) titled "The Importance of Pleasure in Lanyer's 'Description of Cookham.'" One function of such an essay, however, would be to distinguish between the different *kinds* of pleasure the passage explores. These would include not only the specific pleasures already mentioned but also the contrasting pleasures emphasized in lines 13–16. Those lines suggest that the poem is making a sort of argument—an argument suggesting that spiritual pleasures are better and more enduring than mere material pleasures. Thematic critics would then read the rest of the poem with this sort of argument in mind. They would want to see if this kind of argument does indeed help unify the poem as a whole.

MARXIST critics might have a significantly different reaction to this poem than the reaction attributed to Longinus (above). Marxists might argue that this passage reflects the speaker's need to flatter the rich and powerful. They might suggest that whatever the personal character of the Countess of Cumberland herself may have been, she was a powerful person who benefited from an essentially unjust socioeconomic system. Lanyer's speaker, rather than challenging that system or refusing to be a part of it, instead implicitly cooperates with it and thereby strengthens it. Of course, Lanyer would have had little choice about cooperating, especially if she depended on people like the Countess for money, preferment, and access to other powerful people with money.

Moreover, the fact that Lanyer endorses Christian beliefs in this passage and in her poems in general might trouble some Marxists. Many Marxists consider religious belief misguided and self-defeating. They often regard religion as one of the most powerful means (in every sense of the word "powerful") by which the rich dominate the thinking, emotions, and behavior of the lower classes. By focusing attention on the distant past and on some mythical supernatural future, religions distract common people from the need for real, practical change in the here and now. By celebrating the "celestial pleasures" of heaven and denigrating mere "earthly treasures" (15–16), Lanyer's speaker arguably distracts her readers from the real practical value of possessing "earthly treasures," at least if earthly treasures are defined as a decent standard of living for everyone. In addition, Lanyer's speaker arguably deflects attention from the fact that it is the Countess of Cumberland, and the tiny minority of people like her, who actually possess most of the "earthly treasures" that are supposedly so unimportant.

FEMINIST critics might respond in varying ways to this passage. On the one hand, they might appreciate the fact that a literate, intelligent woman is addressing another literate, intelligent, and very powerful woman during a time when unfortunately too few women were literate or powerful, however innately intelligent they may have been. Lanyer, as one of the first published women poets in English history, and as a woman writer who often thought and wrote *as* a woman, might be regarded by many feminists as an important role model for other women, not only of her time but also later. Moreover, because "The Description of Cookham" is one of the very earliest poems written about an English "country house," Lanyer demonstrates not only talent as a poet but talent as a poetic innovator. In this text, she does not simply write the kind of poem that many other poets had already written; instead, she gambles and tries to do something relatively new. Certainly hers was the first "country house poem" actually published in England, and in that respect it surpassed many later, more famous poems by men.

However, while many feminists have applauded Lanyer for all the achievements just mentioned, it is possible to imagine some feminists who might find this poem less than ideal in various ways. For example, the Countess of Cumberland is praised in this passage for "grace" (2). This word had many positive meanings in Lanyer's time, but it might strike some feminists as too tame, too mild, too stereotypically feminine. Moreover, the countess is repeatedly praised for her virtue—but virtue, for the women of her era, could often be a more confining, constricting standard than it was for men. Often, for instance, it revolved around the conventional ideal that women should be "chaste, silent, and obedient." The Countess, by encouraging Lanyer to write, was beginning to challenge that age-old ideal, and Lanyer was also beginning to challenge it by actually writing. Some feminists might be even happier with Lanyer's poem, however, if it were more clearly radical, as some later writings by women definitely would be.

NEW HISTORICIST critics might be especially interested in the ways this poem reflects the complicated power relations of its era. For instance, the speaker's reference to having the "power the virtuous to content" (4) refers most obviously to poetic power or literary talent. But new historicists might note that Lanyer's ability to "content" the "virtuous" depended greatly on her access to literally powerful people such as the Countess of Cumberland. It would not at all surprise new historicists that Lanyer feels the need to thank the "great Lady" who was the "Mistress" of Cookham (11). Such gratitude is not a case of simple good manners but an implied acknowledgment of the Countess's social and economic power and of her ability to favor and support Lanyer in the future. Indeed, a new historicist might argue that although this excerpt seems to focus on benefits and patronage given in the past, part of Lanyer's real concern is with ensuring that such patronage continues into the future. The excerpt helps benefit the Countess by widely advertising her virtue, her kindness, her exemplary Christianity, and her support of the arts. New historicists might respond to the details of the poem in much the same way as Marxists, although without feeling any great need to turn the excerpt to any present political use. In fact, one difference between new historicists and Marxists (or "cultural materialists") is that the latter usually adopt a particular current political agenda. Marxists and cultural materialists often fault new historicists for failing to do the same. Thus, new historicists might be content simply to study the complex power relations reflected in this excerpt, whereas Marxists or cultural materialists might use this excerpt to make political arguments about power relations of the present day.

10

Ben Jonson (1572–1637):

"On My First Son"; "To Penshurst" (excerpt)

Ben Jonson was one of the most important writers of his era. Poet, dramatist, and leading writer of "masques" (elaborate entertainments for the royal court), he especially flourished during the reign of King James I (1603–25). His works were mainly intended to praise virtue and condemn vice, but sometimes their purposes were more personal, as in this deeply tender poem on the death of his first son, who died from the plague at age seven.

ON MY FIRST SON

Farewell, thou child of my right hand, and joy;
My sin was too much hope of thee, lov'd boy.
Seven years thou wert lent to me, and I thee pay,
Exacted by thy fate, on the just day.
O, could I lose all father now! For why   [5]
Will man lament the state he should envy?
To have so soon 'scap'd world's and flesh's rage,
And if no other misery, yet age?
Rest in soft peace, and, ask'd, say, "Here doth lie
Ben Jonson his best piece of poetry."   [10]

For whose sake henceforth all his vows be such,
As what he loves may never like too much.

ARISTOTLE might value Jonson's poem because it satisfies so many of Aristotle's requirements for a successful poem. It suggests complex and enduring truths about humans, especially about the love of parents for their children. It thus implies the existence of a general human nature, so that the poem seems as relevant today as when it was written. The poem also reveals Jonson's talent in using the classical genre known as the epigram, which was typically expected to be short, clear, and pointed, particularly at the end. Jonson, in the final line of his epigram, includes subtle word-play involving "loves" and "like" (where "like" seems to mean "please," although other meanings are also possible). Throughout the poem, in fact, clever phrasing is used. Jonson's son, for instance, was himself named "Benjamin," which in Hebrew literally means "son of the right hand," although the Biblical child eventually known as Benjamin was originally given a name that meant "son of my sorrow." By calling his child the son of his right hand, Jonson implies the boy's special value while also preparing for the later idea that Benjamin was his father's "best piece of poetry" (10). Further subtle phrasing occurs when Jonson says that he wishes he could "lose all father" (5). This phrase, in one sense, expresses a yearning to forget all paternal feelings. But because "lose" in the original printing was spelled "loose," it could mean to let loose (or give vent to) all those feelings, while the verb could also suggest a desire to be freed from all such feelings. Here and in many other ways, Jonson demonstrates the kind of careful poetic craftsmanship that Aristotle so highly valued.

PSYCHOANALYTIC critics might see the father's "hope" and "sin" (2) as expressing his selfish id—his desire for individual satisfaction. In this sense the child symbolizes personal self-assertion. (After all, the poem nowhere mentions the child's mother.) The fact that the dead child is a boy also seems significant: had he lived, he would presumably have perpetuated his father's surname. In this poem (psychoanalytic critics might contend) the ego attempts to find order and meaning in (or to impose them on) a painful, apparently meaningless loss. Arguably, the poem powerfully and convincingly embodies the conflicts between the speaker's emotional id (1 and 5), rational ego (3–4 and 7), and moralistic superego (2–4, especially in the references to sin and justice). By escaping the "flesh's rage" (7), the boy has escaped (among other troubles) the forceful sexual urges accompanying puberty. Indeed, the poem itself can be seen as expressing rage at the flesh—not only at the limits and impermanence of individual bodies but also at the inevitable frustration of the id's fleshly desires. In finally vowing never again to "like too much," the speaker tries to use reason to control his emotions and his future. The speaker attempts to respond reasonably (by exercising the rational ego) to a painful emotional loss (felt mainly by the irrational id).

ARCHETYPAL critics might argue that this poem confronts such common human fears as those of death, the unknown, separation from a loved one, and offending a higher power. The poem arguably draws on widespread human desires for security, love, control of the future, and immortality. Children seem archetypally innocent and symbolize new beginnings. Thus a child's death usually seems especially tragic and particularly unfair. Archetypally, sons (especially first sons) have often been seen as crucial to their parents, especially to their fathers. A son's death therefore also implies one's own death, so that a child's death can make mortality seem doubly destructive. Moreover, the fact that this poem emphasizes a *father's* loss is archetypally significant, since fathers have often been associated archetypally with dominion, control, order, wisdom, and authority. Jonson, however, must try to regain control and must struggle to assert (or accept) wisdom. He must, in a sense, face becoming a son again. He must not only acknowledge but also accept God's greater wisdom. Most basically, the poem deals with the inevitable archetypal experience of dealing with any great loss or disappointment.

DIALOGICAL critics might argue that the poem articulates various, sometimes competing voices. The speaker engages in explicit or implicit dialogue with himself, God, his son, his readers (including other fathers, other parents, other Christians, etc.), and a variety of literary, poetic, and philosophical traditions. His tones are sometimes gentle and loving (1 and 9), sometimes self-accusing (2), sometimes logically rational (3–4), sometimes exasperated and frustrated (5), sometimes self-consoling (7–8), sometimes modestly proud (9–10), and sometimes resolutely stoic (11–12). The interactions among these voices and tones might sometimes seem a civilized dialogue, sometimes a heated debate. Although in one sense the poem is highly personal, in another it is insistently rhetorical. The speaker seeks to persuade both his readers and himself. Dialogical critics might say that the fact that no single voice triumphs may actually contribute to the poem's moral and intellectual integrity and artistic success. From start to finish, then, the poem is obsessed with speech—with questions, answers, exclamations, declarations, and vows. MULTICULTURAL critics might at first find this poem uninteresting. It seems to draw on (and appeal to) emotions so basic and fundamental—so generically "human"—that political or social differences might almost seem irrelevant. Yet it could be argued that Jonson is able to transcend such "marginal" concerns precisely by situating himself near the center of some of his culture's dominant values. Obviously, for instance, he speaks as a successful (if momentarily disappointed) heterosexual male. However, one need not assume that his poem would be unappealing to gay men or lesbians. Indeed, they might even be especially attracted to a work celebrating a love that combines deep affection and wholehearted cultural approval. Or they particularly sympathize with a speaker who feels painfully cut off from the object of his affection. Or they might feel special empathy for a speaker whose desire to raise a child has been denied by "fate" (or a higher power.) Certainly most heterosexuals in Jonson's culture would have been able to identify strongly with the poem's speaker, and any bisexuals would presumably have had even more complicated reactions to the epigram than "straights" or "gays."

In this poem, Jonson speaks as both a heterosexual male and a Christian. In these senses, he belonged to two of his society's most powerful social groups. The fact that the poem betrays little evidence of his Roman Catholic faith may merely reflect, again, its indifference to "irrelevant" distinctions, its focus on more "basic" emotions and values. There can be no doubt, however, that Jonson would generally have been able to write more freely if his Catholicism had been tolerated (or even sanctioned) by his larger culture. We can only imagine how this epigram might have differed if he had been able to practice open Catholicism (or Judaism, or Hinduism, or any other non-Christian faith) in the England of his day. Surely a Jew or Moslem would be able to identify with the sentiments Jonson expresses, but just as surely those sentiments would have been expressed in subtly different ways. Of course, if Jonson had lived in London as an African slave, or as an American Indian, or even as an English atheist, his life and work would probably have differed greatly. Although this epigram seems mostly silent about multicultural issues, multiculturalists would nonetheless explore the ways Jonson's poem and life silently took such issues for granted.

From To Penshurst

"To Penshurst" is a lengthy poem (consisting of 102 lines) written to celebrate the estate of the Sidney family and to extol that family's virtues. The great author and courtier Sir Philip Sidney (see Chapter 4) had been born on the estate, although he was long dead when Jonson wrote this poem. Philip's younger brother Sir Robert Sidney was now the current owner of the house and grounds. Jonson respected the extended Sidney family partly because they valued (and often wrote) literature themselves. Robert Sidney and his wife also treated Jonson with real esteem, not only inviting him to stay overnight at their home but also treating him as a very welcome guest. "To Penshurst" expresses gratitude for their kindness and courtesy, but the poem also implicitly contrasts ancient, venerable Penshurst (which seems an archetypal "home") with the newly constructed mansions of other contemporary aristocrats (which seem mere "houses," no matter how much their construction cost). In the following passage, Jonson, having already discussed all the varied wildlife living on the estate, now describes its vegetation as well as the peasants and commoners who live nearby.

> Then hath thy orchard fruit, thy garden flowers,
>   Fresh as the air, and new as are the hours.   [40]
> The early cherry, with the later plum,
>   Fig, grape, and quince, each in his time doth come;
> The blushing apricot and woolly peach
>   Hang on thy walls, that every child may reach.
> And though thy walls be of the country stone,   [45]
>   They're reared with no man's ruin, no man's groan;
> There's none that dwell about them wish them down;
>   But all come in, the farmer and the clown,

And no one empty-handed, to salute
   Thy lord and lady, though they have no suit.   [50]
Some bring a capon, some a rural cake,
   Some nuts, some apples; some that think they make
The better cheeses bring them, or else send
   By their ripe daughters, whom they would commend
This way to husbands, and whose baskets bear   [55]
   An emblem of themselves in plum or pear . . .

LONGINUS might admire this passage because of all the lofty virtues and virtuous conditions it implicitly and explicitly celebrates. These include careful stewardship of nature (39), concern for the welfare of children (44), a refusal to exploit fellow humans (46), harmonious social relations (47), a welcoming attitude toward neighbors (48), gratitude and courtesy (49–50), generosity (51–3), and an endorsement of marriage. In this passage and throughout the poem, Jonson extols a place of material abundance while never seeming merely materialistic. Indeed, he makes Penshurst symbolize the opposite of such attitudes as materialism, greed, envy, lust, ostentation, and pride (to mention just a few). Penshurst is presented as an almost Edenic setting; it represents the kind of life humans once lived and might ideally still live if they were motivated by the proper values and aspirations. Appropriately, the poem ends by emphasizing deeply spiritual ideals—ideals that Longinus would have prized as suggesting some of the best moral standards humans can achieve. Surely Longinus would admire the ways this poem arguably encourages all humans to be the best they can ethically and spiritually be.

THEMATIC critics emphasize the main "themes" or key ideas that are either explicit or merely implied in literary texts. By repeatedly stressing certain major motifs (these critics believe), a text achieves not only artistic unity but also coherence as a form of argument. One major theme reiterated in "To Penshurst," for instance, is the motif of harmony between humans and nature. This idea (and ideal) can be detected in a surprising number of the poem's lines. It appears, for example, in line 40's references to an "orchard" and "gardens." Orchards are designed by humans to make nature as productive as possible in providing the "fruit" humans eat as food. Similarly, gardens are arranged by humans to be as abundant as possible in displaying the beauty of flowers, since humans value beauty as well as physical nourishment. In this line as so often elsewhere, Jonson also implies the themes of order and balance, which are both partly rooted in humanity's stewardship of nature. Thus the orchards at Penshurst provide fruits that ripen each in their proper times (41–2), so that the humans who live on the estate never lack nourishment. The owners of the estate have even taken pains to ensure that some trees are planted right against the walls of the estate, so that the trees grow horizontally as well as vertically (a technique still practiced at Penshurst today). Children can thus reach the fruit easily (44)—another example of the cooperation between humans and nature at the Sidney estate. Indeed, practically every line of this excerpt suggests some kind of union of humans and nature. Thus, local stones are used to construct the estate's walls (45); farmers, who till the land, are welcome guests at Penshurst (48); the local commoners make gifts for the Sidneys out of natural products (51–3); and even the farmers' marriageable daughters are likened to ripe fruit (54–6). The theme of humans in harmony with nature is one of the most all-pervasive motifs in the entire poem.

MARXIST critics might question (and indeed *have* questioned) the idealization of the Sidneys and the Sidney estate that so many readers have seen in "To Penshurst." The Sidneys, after all, were aristocrats who benefited from a socioeconomic system that most Marxists would consider inherently unjust. It was the Sidneys who owned the orchards and gardens that the poem praises, and it was the Sidneys who were able to purchase a massive house and who benefited, first and foremost, from all the plants, livestock, wildlife, fish, and other animals Jonson describes. The claim that the walls of the Sidney estate were "reared with no man's ruin, no man's groan" and that "There's none that dwell about them wish them down" (46–7) strikes many Marxists as either naïve or deliberately untruthful. Jonson, who worked as a bricklayer himself in his youth, would have known how hard such physical labor could be. Marxists might claim that it seems unlikely that *none* of the commoners living near the Sidney estate resented the wealth and privilege that the Sidneys enjoyed, especially when so many "farmer[s]" and "clown[s]" had so many fewer possessions and opportunities than the Sidneys. Marxists might argue that Jonson, whether deliberately or through mere wishful thinking, "mystifies" and simplifies the actual complexity of relations between the rich and the poor (or relatively poor) on and near the Sidney estate. The commoners who visit the Sidneys and who bring them gifts may have felt obligated, at least to some degree, to do so. Many of them were probably tenant farmers. In fact, some critics have even suggested that the farmers' most obvious reason for visiting the Sidneys would have been to pay their yearly rents, either in the form of cash or in the form of crops and produce. Marxists might appreciate Jonson's criticism of greed and materialism elsewhere in the poem, but they might suggest that the Sidneys were probably far from completely innocent of such motives themselves.

MULTICULTURAL critics, like Marxists, might be suspicious of the ways Jonson seems to present life at Penshurst as one of harmony and homogeneity. Peasants, commoners, and workers are described in ways that minimize their differences from the Sidneys and that also minimize distinctions among themselves. The ethos of the entire poem, for instance, seems thoroughly heterosexual. Jonson emphasizes the sexual fertility of the animals and plants on the estate as well as of the Sidneys themselves. Part of the whole point of life at Penshurst seems to be heterosexual reproduction. Thus it is far from surprising that this excerpt emphasizes the presence of "ripe," marriageable daughters, who have come to Penshurst (partly at the urging of their parents) to display themselves to potential husbands (54–5). The poem simply takes for granted—and thus helps perpetuate—a larger cultural emphasis on heterosexuality and on sexual reproduction. Marriage (a relationship from which gays were until recently absolutely excluded) is extolled both in this passage and near the very end of the poem. In this poem, as in so much literature from the Renaissance, gays are conspicuous by their absence, and, in the few texts in which homosexual relations are mentioned, they are usually strongly condemned. This poem might interest a multicultural critic less for what it says than for what it does *not* say or for what it implies. One message it seems to take for granted is that same-sex desire is rarely important enough even to be touched upon in most Renaissance texts.

ECOCRITICS, with their emphasis on relations between humans and nature, might be interested in the entirety of "To Penshurst," which was one of the first and certainly the most influential of all the "country house poems" written in the seventeenth century. They might note how the poem draws on and perpetuates a whole tradition, in classical literature, of "pastoral" and "georgic" poems that stress the roles of humans interacting in and with a natural landscape. Jonson's poem highlights the ancient Judaeo-Christian idea of humans as stewards of God's creation, placed in lordship over the land and over living creatures. People were expected to use these gifts for their own benefit and for God's glory. The creation of orchards and gardens (39) might be seen, at least by some ecocritics, as evidence of a balanced, sustainable relationship between humans and nature—a relationship that does not involve rape of the land, plunder of the seas, or the fouling of air and waters through massive pollution. Penshurst, an ecocritic might argue, symbolizes a sane, humane approach to the environment. Even when Jonson alludes earlier in the poem to the deaths of animals, he minimizes (or perhaps naïvely ignores) their suffering and pain (20–38). In some ways his depiction of the relations between humans and nature at Penshurst seems too good to be true, but it was probably never intended to be strictly realistic. Rather, it was intended to symbolize the kind of harmony humans had once enjoyed with their environment (before the fall) and the kind they might partially reclaim through proper godly behavior. Part of the appeal of this symbolism in Jonson's era probably involved the ways the lifestyle celebrated in "To Penshurst" contrasted with the lifestyle evident in such rapidly growing cities as London, which were increasingly packed with people and pollution. Some ecocritics might value Jonson's poem for implying environmental goals human might strive to achieve, although other ecocritics might regard the poem as hopelessly romantic and unrealistic.

11

Lady Mary Wroth (1587–1651/3):

"Like to the Indians"

Like to the Indians

This poem is part of a sonnet sequence included in Wroth's *The Countesse of Montgomeries Urania* (1621), an extremely lengthy work combining prose and verse. Wroth, who by birth was part of the distinguished Sidney family (see Chapters 4 and 11), here shows the continuing popularity of love sonnets in England—a popularity largely touched off, decades earlier, by the success of Sir Philip Sidney's *Astrophil and Stella* sonnet sequence. The speaker of the present poem is Pamphilia, the chief female character of the larger work.

22.

Like to the Indians scorched with the Sunne,
    The Sunne which they doe as their God adore:
    So am I us'd by Love, for evermore
    I worship him, lesse favours have I wonne.

Better are they who thus to blacknesse run,   [5]
    And so can onely whitenesse want deplore:

Then I who pale and white am with griefes store,
Nor can have hope, but to see hopes undone.

Besides their sacrifice receiv'd in sight,
   Of their chose Saint, mine hid as worthlesse rite,   [10]
Grant me to see where I my offerings give.

Then let me weare the marke of Cupids might,
   In heart, as they in skin of Phoebus light,
Not ceasing offerings to Love while I live.

HORACE, the ancient Roman poet whose writings had an enormous impact on Renaissance literature, believed that writers, to be popular, should write with the interests and preferences of their actual audiences in mind. Wroth, in this sonnet, does just that. She does so partly by using the sonnet form (which was enormously popular in this period) and also by writing about the topic of love (one of the favorite themes of Renaissance poets and their audiences). But Horace also believed that authors should not slavishly imitate their predecessors. Instead, they should innovate in moderate and acceptable (not extreme and unappealing) ways. Wroth innovates in just this fashion, partly because the speaker of this poem is a woman, not a male (as most readers would have expected in a sonnet sequence). Wroth thus makes her poem interesting to as wide a readership as possible, appealing not only to male readers but to females as well. Horace would have approved of this broad appeal. In addition, her poem follows custom (an important Horatian criterion) by presenting a speaker who feels subservient to an ungrateful Cupid (referred to here as "Love"). By writing this poem, Wroth also meets several other important Horatian standards. First, she offers some general insight into human nature (suggesting, for instance, the widespread power of desire). Second, she uses language that would, in practically every way, have been accessible to her readers, not only because it is relatively simple but also because it discusses highly conventional topics. And, last but not least, her poem reveals her artistic skill, especially in the way she successfully uses the standard rhyme scheme of a Petrarchan sonnet, as well as in the way she develops a single main comparison (of her speaker to Indians) over the entire course of the poem.

ARCHETYPAL critics believe that the most powerful literature appeals to the most profound, most common, most universal human desires and fears. These emotions allegedly transcend the relatively unimportant limits of time, place, gender, race, ethnicity, religion, culture, and so on. They are universal and are rooted in a deep, widely shared human nature. Wroth's poem might interest archetypal critics because it seems to take for granted various extremely common human traits. These include the desire to worship either a god or something equally powerful; the almost irresistible force of love or desire; the tendency to compare one's own situation to the situations of others; the impulse to appeal to higher powers when in need; frustration with ingratitude or injustice, and so on. Archetypal critics would argue that although Cupid (referred to here as "Love") is a deity invented by the Greeks and Romans and well known to people of the Renaissance, almost all humans, everywhere, can relate to the idea that romantic desire is an exceptionally powerful impulse that can even seem as powerful as a god.

MULTICULTURAL critics, unlike archetypal critics, emphasize differences between humans, rather than similarities. In particular, they emphasize differences of race, gender, ethnicity, religion, culture, and so on. The mere fact that Wroth's poem mentions "Indians" (1) and non-Christian forms of worship would interest multicultural critics, as would the fact that the poem is written by a woman and features a female speaker. The poem acknowledges racial and cultural differences in ways that were not particularly common in Renaissance poetry. It thereby reflects the ways early modern European cultures were changing as they became increasingly aware of cultures and ways of life distant from Europe and different from European practices. Interestingly, however, Wroth's speaker assumes that black people "deplore" their "want" (or lack) of white skins (6), as if whiteness were the preferred ideal rather than an unimportant detail. Arguably, then, the poem implies the racism or sense of racial superiority of Wroth's speaker and of many other white Europeans. They could compare themselves with persons of colors in some ways (as Wroth's speaker does in lines 1–4), but they fundamentally assumed that being white was preferable to being nonwhite. Wroth's poem treats dark skin color as an unfortunate, regrettable side-effect of worshipping the sun rather than as a trait to value and be proud of.

POSTMODERN critics question explanations and claims to truth often taken for granted by others. Like deconstructors, they look for evidence of irresolvable contradictions and paradoxes. They are more interested in any evidence of "chaos" rather than of order. They are also interested in any aspect of a literary work that is unexpected, unconventional, and untraditional. Postmodernists might therefore be interested in Wroth's poem for many of the same reasons that this poem might interest multicultural critics. These include the facts that its author and speaker are both women and that it alludes to non-Europeans peoples and cultures. These features make the poem relatively unconventional, especially as a Renaissance sonnet. The poem makes clear that different peoples worship different gods. The mere acknowledgment of that fact might conceivably create skepticism about the Christian god. The recognition that there are multiple forms of worship might (and did) lead increasing numbers of early modern people to doubt the validity of any religion at all. Interestingly, Wroth's speaker suggests that differences of skin color are literally superficial: they result from different amounts of exposure to the sun. Rather than being evidence of any truly fundamental differences between races, different skin colors (Wroth's speaker seems to suggest) are trivial. This poem can thus be read as undermining any "grand narrative" implying immutable racial differences. Alternatively, it could be read (by Renaissance Christians) as implying that both the speaker and the "Indians" she mentions (1) worship false, disappointing gods. If read this way, the poem might be seen as confirming the Christian grand narrative—an outcome postmodernists would not relish.

ECOCRITICS, with their interest in sustainable relations between humans and nature, might be interested in Wroth's allusions to dark-skinned Indians—presumably the kinds of "Indians" that had recently been discovered in the Americas by Columbus and other explorers. The claim that these Indians worship the sun might make them seem literally more in contact with nature than light-skinned European Christians, who worshipped a god who is literally supernatural. Although the poem does not explicitly depict the Indians as nature-worshippers, such worship can reasonably be inferred. After all, they honor one of the most important components of nature (the sun), without which most other forms of life would not be possible. Presumably their worship of the sun involves acknowledging the sun's crucial role in human agriculture, including the part it plays in the transition from one season to the next. Sun-worshippers, almost by definition, would take seriously humanity's dependence on nature. For all these reasons, ecocritics might find Wroth's emphasis on humans in close touch with nature to be worth their time and attention.

Martha Moulsworth (1577–1646): "The Memorandum of Martha Moulsworth, Widow" (excerpt)

Martha Moulsworth wrote her poetic "Memorandum" in 1632, when she was fifty-five years of age. By that time she had been married and widowed three times. She had given birth to a number of children, all of whom predeceased her. Her poem is remarkable not only as one of the first autobiographies by anyone, especially a woman, in the English language but also because of her extremely unusual call for higher education for women, including the establishment of a women's university.

THE MEMORANDUM OF MARTHA MOULSWORTH, WIDOW (excerpt)

In carnal state of sin original
I did not stay one whole day natural;
The seal of grace in sacramental water
So soon had I, so soon become the daughter
Of earthly parents and of heavenly father.   [15]
Some christen late for state, the wiser rather [i.e, earlier].

My name was Martha; Martha took much pain*
Our savior Christ (her guest) to entertain.
God Give me grace my inward house to dight
That he with me may sup, and stay all night.*   [20]

My father was a man of spotless fame,
Of gentle birth, and Dorsett was his name.
He had (and left) lands of his own possession;
He was of Levi's tribe by his profession.

His mother, Oxford, knowing well his worth,   [25]
Arrayed in scarlet robe did send him forth.
By him I was brought up in godly piety,
In modest cheerfulness, and sad sobriety.
Nor only so: beyond my sex and kind
He did with learning Latin deck [my] mind.   [30]
And why not so? The muses females are
And therefore of us females take some care.
Two universities we have of men;
Oh that we had but one of women then!
Oh then that would in wit and tongues surpass   [35]
All art of men that is or ever was!
But I of Latin have no cause to boast:*
For want of use, I long ago it lost.

** MOULSWORTH'S OWN MARGINAL CITATIONS: *Line 17:*
"Luke 10:14." *Line 20:* "Revel[ation] 3[:] 20 / Luke 24:29." *Line
38:* "Latin is not the most / marketable marriage / metal."

ARISTOTLE, with his interest in careful craftsmanship and
complex unity, would find much to admire in this excerpt from
Moulsworth's poem. In this section and throughout the work,
Moulsworth uses language that is carefully balanced both in
phrasing and in concepts, as in lines 15, 16, 18, 23, and various
other examples. Thus the beginning of line 31 echoes but transforms
the beginning of line 29, and in line 28 "modest cheerfulness" is
balanced against "sad sobriety."

In fact, the entire poem is very carefully designed, with fifty-
five couplets to symbolize the fifty-five years of Moulsworth's
life. Similarly, many references to the literal seasons of the year
symbolize the different metaphorical seasons in her life. Above
all, however, Moulsworth enjoys placing phrases or words in
balance with one another, as when she calls herself the daughter
both "Of earthly parents and of heavenly father" (15). The total
effect of her poem is one of firm balance, poise, and equilibrium:
she comes across as a woman who both feels and thinks, who is
both emotional and practical, and who suffers pain while also
appreciating joy. In general, she seems to be a human being who
has been able to achieve a good deal of steadiness and composure
in her life despite the various trials she has faced. Her entire poem
implies the importance of reason, sanity, and good sense, and the

very phrasing and structure of the poem demonstrate all three of these traits. Aristotle might admire both the careful design of the poem itself and the great good sense of the personality it reveals.

FEMINIST critics, in particular, would be especially interested in Moulsworth's "Memorandum." Her text, after all, is one of the very first poems in English in which a woman (1) tells in detail the story of her own life; (2) calls for the creation of a university for women; and (3) reflects in general on the plight of women in her society and era. The relatively recent discovery and recovery of Moulsworth's poem (it was first printed in 1994) reflect the kind of archival scholarship that feminists have long called for. Feminists want to ensure that the voices of women (especially women of the past) are not overlooked. Moulsworth's poem has now been widely reprinted and has been discussed in various books and scholarly essays, making it a prime example of the way feminism has helped broaden and deepen the literary canon.

Yet it is Moulsworth's comments on the status of women in her society that would surely intrigue feminists the most. Thus she emphasizes the crucial role her father played, in a patriarchal society, in making sure she was educated. (Her mother is barely mentioned in the poem.) Her father was one of a small but increasing number of influential men in this period who believed that daughters should have a chance to develop their minds. Moulsworth's call for establishing a women's university would have seemed radical when the poem was first written. Even more radical was her confidence that women could not only intellectually compete with men but actually surpass them in learning. Yet feminists would also note that Moulsworth herself never actually fulfilled her dream of public intellectual achievement; instead (as the rest of the poem makes clear) she was relatively content to play (quite well) the more traditional roles of devoted wife and loving mother. For feminists, then, Moulsworth's poem might be taken as evidence of the ambitions women were beginning to feel but also of the real practical limitations they still faced.

READER-RESPONSE critics might argue that reactions to Moulsworth's poem would depend very much on the particular traits of the readers who encountered it. Women readers might be especially interested in this text for all the reasons just mentioned. Christian readers might also find the poem especially interesting, whereas atheist or agnostic readers might find it far less worth their time—unless, that is, they were curious about history or interested in literature *as* literature. Intellectually ambitious women (or such persons in general) might be able to relate to Moulsworth's desire for higher education, whereas persons less interested in education might be less interested in her hopes and dreams for a women's university. Persons deeply familiar with the Bible would be able to catch most of her biblical allusions without needing to rely on marginal notes, while persons relatively unfamiliar with Christian scriptures would appreciate the help those notes provide. Women (or persons in general) who enjoyed close relations with their fathers might take a special interest in this excerpt. And so on. In short, one's response to this text (or any text) might be deeply affected by one's particular personal traits, background, and sense of identity. There would be no single, "correct" response to this passage; readers' differing responses would be affected by their different individual characteristics.

DIALOGICAL critics are interested in the ways texts present and engage in dialogue involving different voices, tones of voice, or other texts. The excerpt from Moulsworth's "Memorandum" is full of such dialogue. The numerous biblical allusions, for instance, show her echoing the most important text in her culture, thus giving added legitimacy and authority to her own poem. By echoing the voice of God (the most important male voice of her time), she immediately disarms any critics who might have been troubled by a woman writing a poem as radical, in some ways, as her poem is. She immediately and emphatically demonstrates that she is a good, sincere Christian whose values and motives are deeply religious, and she essentially cites allegiance not only to her heavenly father but also to her earthly father before making her unexpected claims for the rights of women. Yet Moulsworth's own tones of voice are intriguingly diverse and complex. Thus, for the first thirty lines of her poem she seems sober, learned, devout, and obedient. But then, in line 31, her tone becomes suddenly more abrupt, emphatic, and quite literally questioning. Anticipating an objection to the idea that a woman should be taught Latin, she tersely asks, "And why not so?" Within a few lines she is using exclamations ("Oh . . . Oh") and exclamation points to emotionally emphasize her arguments (34–6). But no sooner does she assert the fundamental rights and intellectual potential of women than she admits (dejectedly?) that her own ability to speak Latin has long since become a thing of the past (37–8). Finally, the tone of the last marginal note here can be read as simultaneously humorous, sardonic, wistful, and realistic. It also makes a pun, since "latten" in Moulsworth's time was a kind of cheap brass. This one marginal note, then, exemplifies many of the different kinds of tones of voice a talented writer could pack into just a few words. In this excerpt and throughout the poem, Moulsworth's voice is never simple, singular, or literally monotonous. Her tones vary greatly, and she engages in a kind of extended dialogue not only with other texts but also with her imagined, anticipated readers.

NEW HISTORICIST critics are especially interested in issues of power and in how any "text" at all—any bit of cultural residue, whether it be a play by Shakespeare or a list of groceries—can provide insights into the complicated, constantly evolving culture that helped produce it. Moulsworth's poem would interest new historicist critics for all these reasons. The selected excerpt, for instance, instantly reveals a great deal about the culture in which Moulsworth found herself embedded. Clearly that culture was Christian and patriarchal. It placed great value on virtue, piety, property, propriety, knowledge of Latin, and learning in general, but it assumed that only men were entitled to a college education. The excerpt from Moulsworth's poem reflects all these assumptions, but it does more than reflect her culture—it also challenges and intervenes in that culture, dissenting from it in various ways and trying to change it. New historicists typically claim that this emphasis on *interaction* rather than mere *reflection* is one of the traits that helps distinguish their approach from that of more traditional historical critics. According to new historicists, traditional historicists tended to see a work of literature as a mere reflection of its "historical context," whereas new historicists instead assert that there is no single, simple historical "context" but rather many different "contexts" in conflict and competition with each other. While a traditional historical critic might have tended to emphasize people in positions of power (such as monarchs, aristocrats, wealthy persons, and politically influential figures), new historicists are far more likely to explore the lives of people like Moulsworth—a relatively unknown woman, a commoner, someone residing more on the margins of society than in any center of power. New historicism shares with feminism and multiculturalism an interest in persons who might earlier have been overlooked in scholarly studies—people whose lives might earlier have not seemed important or powerful enough to merit academic attention, especially if those people were creative writers. Moulsworth's life and poem reflect and contributed to changes that were taking place in her culture even as she wrote, although—in a paradox new historicists would seize on—the poem never participated widely in the culture of its time because it lay unpublished for well over 300 years. When it *was* finally rediscovered and printed for the first time, it instantly became part of the complicated cultural give-and-take of the very late twentieth century.

12

George Herbert
(1593–1633):

"Redemption";
"The Collar"

George Herbert is widely considered to be one of the greatest
religious poets of the English language. Born into a prominent family,
he distinguished himself academically at Cambridge University and
could easily have become an influential person in either the secular
or the religious hierarchies of his time. Instead, he chose duty as a
country parson at a small church far from the glories of London.
He served his parish faithfully, writing poems in his spare time,
until illness caused his far-too-early death. Nearly all his poems are
meditations on religious topics.

REDEMPTION

Having been tenant long to a rich lord,
   Not thriving, I resolvèd to be bold,
   And make a suit unto him, to afford
A new small-rented lease, and cancel th' old.

In heaven at his manor I him sought;   [5]
   They told me there that he was lately gone

About some land, which he had dearly bought
Long since on earth, to take possessiòn.

I straight returned, and knowing his great birth,
  Sought him accordingly in great resorts;   [10]
  In cities, theaters, gardens, parks, and courts;
At length I heard a ragged noise and mirth

Of thieves and murderers; there I him espied,
Who straight, *Your suit is granted*, said, and died.

HORACE, one of the few prominent theorists of poetry who was himself a practicing and highly successful poet, was concerned first and foremost that authors should write in ways that would win them readers. This meant that their works should be accessible, generally clear, relatively customary, and as pleasing to as wide a variety of readers as possible. They should use forms with which readers were familiar; present characters who were credible human beings; depict situations to which readers could relate; and, in general, not depart too radically from traditional ways of thinking and writing.

Herbert's poetry in general satisfies all of Horace's criteria, and "Redemption" is no exception. The poem's language is simple and lucid. Its story is easy to follow and understand. Its form is the familiar form of the sonnet. Its meaning is readily comprehended by all Christians or by anyone familiar with the basic tenets of Christianity. Finally, the poem's method is that of a parable—a method often used by Jesus himself. Rather than being long, complicated, and full of arcane language and imagery (as is sometimes the case in the works of Herbert's fellow "metaphysical poet," John Donne), Herbert's poetry is almost always immediately intelligible. But its surface simplicity often hides richer meanings when his work is more closely examined.

Everything this poem describes would have been immediately familiar to Herbert's first readers, and much of it remains immediately comprehensible to readers today. The idea of asking a powerful person to renegotiate the terms of a contract is one to which most people can relate, and the behavior of everyone in this poem—the speaker, the "They" employed at the lord's "manor" (5–6), the "thieves and murderers" (13), and, of course, Christ himself (14)—is entirely in character with how one might assume such persons would behave. Herbert innovates, of course, in his retelling of the story of Christ's crucifixion, but he does so in ways that would have offended few if any Christians of his time or later. Indeed, although he wrote during a time of enormous religious controversy, Herbert's verse quickly proved popular with Christians of almost all kinds. Few readers, then or since, have felt that he did any disservice to Christian beliefs, and in fact he has always been one of the most beloved of all Christian poets. Horace was concerned that writers should not offend their audiences or make fools of themselves, and Herbert demonstrably did neither.

MARXIST critics might argue that this poem alludes to real problems—poverty and the suffering of those in need—without offering any real solutions to them. Instead, Herbert refers to an actual, factual situation faced by the vast majority of the people of his time and uses it merely allegorically. That is, he depicts the genuine suffering of physically needy persons simply in order to tell a symbolic story about the need for spiritual redemption. Marxists might argue that this poem exemplifies the ways religion fails to provide real-world answers to real-world problems. The poem also arguably presents this mystical, mythical "rich lord" as being far more compassionate, generous, and self-sacrificing than the real "rich lord[s]" most of Herbert's contemporaries would actually have encountered. If Herbert really hoped to alleviate human suffering (a Marxist might argue), he should not have served as a propagandist for Christianity in general and the Anglican Church in particular. Both Christianity as a system of thought and churches as social institutions (a Marxist might say) did much to retard the progress of the poor and needy. Herbert's poem (a Marxist might argue) inadvertently calls attention to genuine suffering that the poem then essentially ignores.

STRUCTURALIST critics try to offer genuine, objective, almost scientific insights into the ways literature works. They do so by examining the codes of meaning that literary texts imply, reflect, and depend on to be intelligible and meaningful. Learning to "decode" a poem is like learning to understand the words, grammar, and sentence structures of a foreign language. Correct interpretation depends on knowing how the larger code works. For example, it helps to know that this poem is not merely a poem in general but a sonnet, one of the most popular forms of Renaissance poetry and a kind of poetry often associated with secular love. Herbert here adapts the sonnet form to deal with a different, higher kind of love. This poem also alludes to a common social code of Herbert's day—the code associated with tenant farming. Partly the meaning of the poem derives from the way the lord of the manor, at the end of the poem, departs from common behavior according to that well-known code. Instead of refusing to be generous, or instead of being generous in a conventional, expected way, *this* lord surprises us by far exceeding the generosity usually displayed by even the most compassionate landlords of Herbert's day. Everything in the poem, up until the very last line, seems familiar because everything until that line makes sense according to various common codes of Herbert's society. Only in the last line are all these codes overturned. The poem thus illustrates the common structuralist assumption that one of the best ways to communicate emphatically is to violate common expectations.

DECONSTRUCTIVE critics, unlike structuralists, look for gaps and breakdowns in meaning. They assume that no code can be thoroughly and logically consistent. They assume that no interpretation can be final and indisputable. In some ways, Herbert's poem works by setting one code (the code associated with actual tenant farming) against another code (the code associated with the self-sacrificing, astonishingly generous and self-sacrificing love associated with Christ). The Marxist interpretation already offered (see above) goes some distance toward deconstructing this standard Christian way of interpreting Herbert's poem, and for a deconstructor there is no way of deciding *which* of these competing interpretations is correct—the orthodox Christian or the subversively Marxist. Thus, two different kinds of readers can read exactly the same words and arrive at diametrically opposite interpretations. Most traditional theories of interpretation would try to decide which interpretation was "correct," or they would at least try to harmonize or find common ground between the two opposite views. A deconstructor, in contrast, would say that there is no logical way or even need to resolve these kinds of disagreement. The same text is potentially open to endless interpretation in which no interpretation is or ever could be "correct."

NEW HISTORICIST critics, with their interest in all kinds of power relations, might be especially intrigued by what this poem implies about the exercise of power in Herbert's society. On the one hand the poem alludes to the real, hard-nosed social system of tenant farming, in which tenants were obligated to fulfill the terms of their leases or risk losing their lands. Payment—either in cash or in crops—had to be made to the rich lords who rented out the lands that tenant farmers leased. Yet the poem sets this system of real power against a different system. In the latter, the lord who leases us our very existence is willing to die to pay our debts. He is willing to suffer, and to sacrifice himself, to alleviate the suffering of others. One way to read Herbert's poem from a new historcist point of view is to see it as a subtle criticism of the earthly system of tenant farming and indeed as a subtle criticism of all earthly power relations. The poem can be read as an implied rebuke to any landlord who refused to be generous in his dealings with his tenants. Yet any such subversive potential we might find in the poem is, arguably, counteracted by the fact that the meaning of the poem is mainly symbolic and allegorical. Rich, strict, law-abiding landlords in Herbert's day easily could— and usually did—see themselves as devout Christians. Thus any possibility of reading Herbert's poem as a fundamental critique of power relations in his society was "always already" (to use a favorite cliché of recent criticism) contained and controlled and undercut. Potentially subversive meanings had already themselves been subverted.

In "The Collar," a priest (presumably Anglican) laments the many practical sacrifices he has had to make by choosing a life devoted to serving God and other Christians. The poem's title is rich in multiple meanings: the speaker, full of "choler" (or anger), regrets having ever chosen to wear the priestly "collar," but his attitude changes when he hears the voice of the divine Caller addressing him at the very end of the poem.

THE COLLAR

I struck the board, and cried, "No more;
      I will abroad!
What? shall I ever sigh and pine?
My lines and life are free, free as the road,
Loose as the wind, as large as store.   [5]
      Shall I be still in suit?

Have I no harvest but a thorn
To let me blood, and not restore
What I have lost with cordial fruit?
    Sure there was wine   [10]
Before my sighs did dry it; there was corn
Before my tears did drown it.
    Is the year only lost to me?
    Have I no bays to crown it,
No flowers, no garlands gay? All blasted?   [15]
    All wasted?
Not so, my heart; but there is fruit,
    And thou hast hands.
Recover all thy sigh-blown age
On double pleasures: leave thy cold dispute   [20]
Of what is fit and not. Forsake thy cage,
    Thy rope of sands,
Which petty thoughts have made, and made to thee
Good cable, to enforce and draw,
    And be thy law,   [25]
While thou didst wink and wouldst not see.
    Away! take heed;
    I will abroad.
Call in thy death's-head there; tie up thy fears;
    He that forbears   [30]
    To suit and serve his need
    Deserves his load."
But as I raved and grew more fierce and wild
    At every word,
Methought I heard one calling, *Child!*   [35]
    And I replied *My Lord.*

PLATO, with his disdain for uncontrolled emotion and his admiration for reason and morality, might find this poem intriguing in various ways. The speaker, after all, immediately begins by expressing violent emotion, and, as the poem develops, the speaker becomes increasingly "fierce and wild" (33). In other words, he behaves more like an animal and less like a rational human being. His thoughts and behavior seem increasingly selfish. Rather than being content to serve the interests of others, he rejects his obligations to God, the community, and impersonal, lofty ideals. The jagged, unpredictable appearance of the poem on the page, along with its abrupt questions, wild exclamations, and angry questions, all help to convey the sheer irrationality of the speaker. He rebels against authority and reason and shows himself unfit for service, or even participation, in the kind of ideal society Plato sought to fashion and defend in *The Republic*. Only at the very end of the poem does the speaker return to his senses. Called upon directly by God, the source of all goodness and true reason, the speaker suddenly snaps back into rationality, humility, and proper deference to authority. He suddenly begins behaving again as a good Christian—especially a member of the Christian *clergy*—should behave. Plato and Aristotle were widely admired by Christians of Herbert's day as "virtuous pagans" who, simply by relying on the God-given gift of reason, had reached proper conclusions about truth, justice, morality, and proper behavior. Plato's likely response to this poem would therefore resemble the likely response of the many "Christian Platonists" of Herbert's era.

TRADITIONAL HISTORICAL critics might discuss "The Collar," first of all, by explaining how it reflects many of the most common ideas of the time, especially the idea that humans were created by God, shared with God the ability to reason, were expected to use that ability in guiding their thoughts and conduct, and were thus expected to distinguish themselves from lower animals who lacked the full gift of reason. Herbert's speaker, by giving in to his passions, lowers himself on the so-called Great Chain of Being. This "chain" was a standard way of explaining the grand hierarchy that structured the entire universe, including all living things, with God at the top, nine orders of angels beneath him, humans in various rankings (both secular and religious) beneath the angels, and so on down the ladder, with animals, plants, and even minerals ranked in various hierarchical patterns.

However, in addition to explaining larger ideas of this sort (ideas crucial to understanding the poem), traditional historical critics would also explain the meanings of various specific words and phrases in the poem. The meanings of some of these, in some cases, have become less obvious since Herbert's day. The triple pun contained in the title of the poem has already been mentioned, but historical critics might note various other instances. For example, "still in suit" in line 6 means "still suing for favors"; lines 7–8 contain an ironic allusion to Christ's crucifixion; and lines 18–19 allude ironically to the behavior of Adam and Eve in the Garden of Eden. (Both of these latter facts would also interest dialogical critics.) In line 22, the phrase "rope of sands" refers to sand passing through an hourglass—a common symbol of mutability and mortality in Herbert's period. Similarly, the reference to a "death's-head" in line 29 also refers to the use of real, painted, or printed skulls in this period to remind people of their ultimate fate. In short, traditional historical critics would try to offer as full an explanation as possible of anything in the poem that might confuse or mislead modern readers. Like structuralist critics, traditional historical critics assume that a commonly understood code of meanings existed at the time Herbert wrote his poem. Part of the job of both historical and structuralist critics is to explain that code to modern readers. (New historicists and other recent theorists, on the other hand, would argue that even during Herbert's era there were competing, even contradictory codes, so that interpretation is never quite as straightforward a process as traditional historicists allegedly assume.)

PSYCHOANALYTIC critics might respond to "The Collar" in ways strongly resembling the responses of Plato. Freudians might suggest, for instance, that this poem features a lengthy irrational outburst rooted in the speaker's unreasonable "id," that God in the final lines symbolizes the speaker's moral, ethical "superego," and that in the poem's very last line the speaker's rational "ego" literally has the last calm, quiescent, obedient words. The poem arguably displays a temper tantrum in which the speaker behaves as a "*Child*" in several senses of the word (35). God, rather than giving in to anger or any other kind of irrational emotion of his own, instead responds with love, thus behaving precisely as one might expect the lofty, virtuous superego to behave. By setting such a good example for the speaker, God reminds the speaker of the importance of rational, loving behavior, thus prompting the speaker to snap back into conformance with reason, order, love, and the law. Lacanian critics, in fact, might suggest that by the end of the poem the speaker has returned to the realm of the "Father," with its controls and dictates and rules. Yet it is also possible to argue that God, in the final lines, somehow embodies the best stereotypical traits of both kinds of parents—the firm discipline imposed by the traditional father figure as well as the loving acceptance and forgiveness often associated with mothers.

READER-RESPONSE critics might suggest that reactions to "The Collar" would depend very much on the traits, backgrounds, and values of different readers or kinds of readers. Some readers might consider the speaker shamefully selfish, while others might easily comprehend his desire for freedom and self-fulfillment. Some readers might consider his final words sane, sensible, and commendable, while others might see them as evidence of weakness and capitulation. God's single word—"*Child!*"—can be read either as stern or loving (or as both), depending on one's attitude toward religion in general and the Christian god in particular. Some priests (or anyone else who has a demanding job involving public service, such as a nurse or doctor or police officer or fire fighter) might very much sympathize with Herbert's speaker. Others, in contrast, might suggest that the priest knew what kind of life he would lead when he decided to become a priest; they might therefore condemn his rejection of responsibilities he freely assumed. Parents with disobedient children (i.e., most parents) might sympathize with God here, while rebellious teenagers might admire the speaker's yearning for freedom and pleasure. In short, the range of possible reactions to this poem is almost as varied as the range of potential readers.

POSTMODERN critics might enjoy the free-wheeling, uninhibited, unpredictable form of this poem. Rather than writing a sonnet or using some other traditional genre, Herbert chose in this poem to make the chaos and disorder of the text's shape match the chaotic, disordered emotions of the speaker. (Ironically, formalists might also admire this perfect match between "content" and form.) Postmodernists might enjoy the fact that the poem—at least at first—suggests the inability of a "grand narrative" (such as Christianity) to do true justice to the real complexities of an actual human life. Postmodernists might admire the speaker's rebelliousness and his refusal to conform. They might therefore be disappointed, however, when he seems, in the final line, to capitulate to God's authority. Or perhaps they might read the ending in a more positive way—as evidence of God's actual refusal to *impose* his authority by harshly rebuking or punishing the wayward speaker. By responding (arguably) with love and forgiveness rather than with harsh discipline, God seems more open-minded, tolerant, and compassionate than he is sometimes presented as being. He is here (at least from one point of view) the god of mercy rather than the god of justice. Formalists and other readers looking for harmony and resolution in works of literature might suggest that "The Collar" achieves both traits in its final lines, but postmodernists—interested in openness, randomness, and incompleteness—might argue that the ending of this work is too abrupt, neat, and superficial to provide a solid sense of genuine closure. According to this way of looking at things, the ending of this poem really resolves nothing; all the problems the poem discusses at such length remain, even after the final word.

13

Robert Herrick (1591–1674):

"Corinna's Going A-Maying"; "To the Virgins, to Make Much of Time"

CORINNA'S GOING A-MAYING

Get up, get up for shame! The blooming morn
 Upon her wings presents the god unshorn.
 See how Aurora throws her fair
 Fresh-quilted colours through the air:
 Get up, sweet slug-a-bed, and see   [5]
 The dew bespangling herb and tree!
Each flower has wept and bow'd toward the east
Above an hour since, yet you not drest;
 Nay! not so much as out of bed?
 When all the birds have matins said   [10]
 And sung their thankful hymns, 'tis sin,
 Nay, profanation, to keep in,
Whereas a thousand virgins on this day
Spring sooner than the lark, to fetch in May.

Rise and put on your foliage, and be seen   [15]
To come forth, like the spring-time, fresh and green,
And sweet as Flora. Take no care
For jewels for your gown or hair:
Fear not; the leaves will strew
Gems in abundance upon you: [20]
Besides, the childhood of the day has kept,
Against you come, some orient pearls unwept.
Come, and receive them while the light
Hangs on the dew-locks of the night:
And Titan on the eastern hill   [25]
Retires himself, or else stands still
Till you come forth! Wash, dress, be brief in praying:
Few beads are best when once we go a-Maying.

Come, my Corinna, come; and coming, mark
How each field turns a street, each street a park, [30]
Made green and trimm'd with trees! see how
Devotion gives each house a bough
Or branch! each porch, each door, ere this,
An ark, a tabernacle is,
Made up of white-thorn neatly interwove,   [35]
As if here were those cooler shades of love.
Can such delights be in the street
And open fields, and we not see 't?
Come, we'll abroad: and let's obey
The proclamation made for May,   [40]
And sin no more, as we have done, by staying;
But, my Corinna, come, let's go a-Maying.

There's not a budding boy or girl this day
But is got up and gone to bring in May.
A deal of youth ere this is come   [45]
Back, and with white-thorn laden home.
Some have despatch'd their cakes and cream,
Before that we have left to dream:
And some have wept and woo'd, and plighted troth,
And chose their priest, ere we can cast off sloth: [50]
Many a green-gown has been given,
Many a kiss, both odd and even:

Many a glance, too, has been sent
From out the eye, love's firmament:
Many a jest told of the keys betraying   [55]
This night, and locks pick'd: yet we're not a-Maying!

Come, let us go, while we are in our prime,
And take the harmless folly of the time!
   We shall grow old apace, and die
   Before we know our liberty.   [60]
   Our life is short, and our days run
   As fast away as does the sun.
And, as a vapour or a drop of rain,
Once lost, can ne'er be found again,
   So when or you or I are made   [65]
   A fable, song, or fleeting shade,
   All love, all liking, all delight
   Lies drown'd with us in endless night.
Then, while time serves, and we are but decaying,
Come, my Corinna, come, let's go a-Maying.   [70]

ARISTOTELIAN critics, who helped inspire the emphasis by modern formalists on a work's complex unity, might admire Herrick's poem for its consistency of tone, characterization, imagery, and argument. The poem's tone, for instance, is consistently energetic, as the sheer number of exclamation and question marks implies. The speaker talks and behaves as we might expect most young men to do; he thus exemplifies Aristotle's belief that different *kinds* of persons act and talk in characteristic, predictable ways. (Thus idea, borrowed, from Aristotle, is also one of Horace's main assumptions.) Nothing in the poem fundamentally changes our first impression of the speaker, although his apparently flippant attitude toward religion in lines 27–42 might momentarily unsettle some readers. By lines 49–50, however, he seems to have returned to more conventional religious views: he advocates for marriage, not mere sex. Thus the section beginning in line 27 and ending at line 50 adds some sense of complexity (but not total inconsistency) to his personality.

   Throughout the poem, Herrick uses imagery of light and nature, and the poem both opens and closes with images of the sun. Initially he emphasizes the sun rising (1–4) and then later suggests the sun setting (62). Such repeated imagery, along with the repeated emphasis on going "a-Maying" at the end of each stanza, helps contribute to the poem's over-all coherence and thereby adds to its general display of careful craftsmanship, a feature of good writing that Aristotle highly valued.

THEMATIC critics, who are interested in a work's central ideas or major motifs, might note that this poem perfectly exemplifies the conventional theme known as "*carpe diem*," the idea that humans should "seize [each] day" available to them since another day is never guaranteed. This idea was very popular in poetry of the English Renaissance, especially in poetry of the first half of the seventeenth century, and it is a recurring motif in Herrick's poetry in particular. All these facts would interest thematic critics, who would compare and contrast Herrick's poem with other *carpe diem* texts (such as those by the Roman poet Horace, who originated that Latin phrase), especially any that may have influenced Herrick's own writings or that might help us better understand the particular features of "Corinna's Going A-Maying." Thematic critics, for instance, might want to compare and contrast Herrick's lyric with Andrew Marvell's very famous *carpe diem* poem "To His Coy Mistress" (see Chapter 15), which is arguably much darker and more ironic in tone than Herrick's text. By juxtaposing different poems dealing with the same general theme, thematic critics would be well-positioned to explain how the same idea is treated by different authors or by the same author in different works. Thematic critics, especially any with an interest in history, might want to know how variously the "*carpe diem*" theme may have been dealt with and responded to in Herrick's day, as well as before his time and also later.

ARCHETYPAL critics emphasize the reactions most human beings share, regardless of differences of culture, era, place, nation, race, gender, class, etc. Such critics might argue that Herrick's poem reflects a very basic human tendency to want to enjoy life while life and youth are still available. The poem might also be seen as articulating basic human desires for shared enjoyment, for erotic courtship, and for taking delight in nature. Most people (archetypal critics might argue) can sympathize and indeed empathize with this speaker's emphasis on the pleasures of beauty (both human and natural) and on the yearning for love, especially physical love. Archetypal critics would argue that most readers would be able to relate to such common human experiences as the beginnings and endings of days, the rapid passage of time, the fear of an unknown future after death, and the sheer joy of simple days passed in happiness with a loved one, especially a loved one to whom one feels a romantic attraction. Most people have had personal experiences with birds, flowers, trees, sleeping, rising from bed, tasting treats, kissing, aging, and indeed practically every other detail mentioned in this text. Little in the poem, then, seems odd or unfamiliar, and so Herrick's lyric might arguably appeal to almost any reader anywhere at any time.

ECOCRITICS emphasize relations between humans and nature, and they especially prize literary works that encourage people to appreciate nature and help ensure its survival. Ecocritics might therefore particularly value Herrick's poem, which celebrates the beauty and value of the natural world from start to finish. In fact, almost by definition *carpe diem* poems focus on the natural world rather than on some supposed supernatural existence, and Herrick's poem specifically ties the happiness of humans in the present to pleasurable interaction with plants, animals, the landscape, and the great outdoors. The speaker urges Corinna not simply to sit back and observe nature but rather to come out into nature and participate in the various pleasures it offers. Any distinctions between human creations and nature are de-emphasized: birds seem to say matins and sing hymns (10–11); virgins behave like larks (13–14); dressing is compared to donning foliage (15); Corinna is compared to a budding flower (15–17); and so on throughout the entire work. Herrick's poem is the kind of text that explicitly makes us appreciate nature and that implicitly encourages us to ensure that nature will always play a major and satisfying role in our lives.

DARWINIAN critics would be surprised by almost nothing in Herrick's poem. After all, this is a work that depicts a young man wooing a young woman in a context that celebrates the wooing of many young women by many young men. Ultimately and ideally, all this wooing leads to engagement and marriage (49–50), and, after that, presumably to procreation and the eventual repetition of this entire cycle. That cycle that has been repeated from one generation to the next since the beginning of human life on this planet. Some Darwinians believe that much art originated as part of courtship rituals—as part of efforts by young men and young women to make themselves attractive to one another or to make themselves seem "special" and worthy of others' attention. Males of various species often "perform" to attract the attention and win the assent of females, and males of various species have even been selected, over countless generations, for features that have consistently won them the attention of females. Thus the peacock has his magnificent tail and male birds of paradise "dance" to win their mates. Similarly (a Darwinian might argue), young men have always had a vested interest in wooing and winning the sexual assent of young women, while young women have long had a vested interest in finding mates who were both talented and committed. Darwinians might see Herrick's poem as one product of desires "hard-wired" into the genes of most men and women—desires essential to human reproduction.

TO THE VIRGINS, TO MAKE MUCH OF TIME

Gather ye rose-buds while ye may,
   Old Time is still a-flying;
And this same flower that smiles today
   Tomorrow will be dying.

The glorious lamp of heaven, the sun,   [5]
   The higher he's a-getting,
The sooner will his race be run,
   And nearer he's to setting.

That age is best which is the first,
   When youth and blood are warmer;   [10]
But being spent, the worse, and worst
   Times still succeed the former.

Then be not coy, but use your time,
   And while ye may, go marry;
For having lost but once your prime,   [15]
   You may forever tarry.

HORACE would almost certainly admire this poem, especially since Horace himself was a key source of much *carpe diem* poetry. Indeed, part of Horace's enormous influence as a poetic theorist derived from his example as an enormously popular poet, not only in his own day but also in subsequent periods. This was especially the case during the Renaissance, and so it is not surprising that Herrick and so many other poets of this era modeled their work not only on Horace's own poems but also on his ideas about poetry. This particular poem, for instance, exhibits many traits Horace endorsed. These include clear, simple diction; a conventional form; conventional ideas; conventional characterization; and at least one adjustment to the mores of the poet's particular audience. Thus, in advising young women to "marry" (14) (rather than merely enjoy physical pleasure), Herrick's speaker makes his poem more acceptable to the Christian readers of his day, particularly the more sober-minded among them.

PSYCHOANALYTIC critics might argue that this poem particularly reflects, and appeals to, the part of the psyche that Freud called the "id"—that is, the part of the unconscious most concerned with enjoying pleasure. The poem justifies the pursuit of pleasure in the here and now, and rather than associating the aging process with (for instance) the growth of wisdom or a receding interest in foolish distractions, Herrick's speaker instead associates aging with a movement from "worse" to "worst" times (11). The one reference to "heaven" fails to mention God (the personification of the superego and the source of all immutable joy); instead, it links heaven to mutability, decay, and descent. Young women are implicitly urged to enjoy the physical pleasures men can afford them, and so the poem can be seen as one of many manifestations of the male "gaze" (which objectifies women) and of male desire. A Freudian might even see the reference to "rose-buds" as an unconscious allusion to female genitalia.

Yet although the poem does seem to celebrate physical pleasure as an ideal, one can also read it as reflecting, in part, the influence of both the ego and the superego. The ego is the aspect of the mind that tries to deal realistically with things as they actually are, while the superego is the aspect of the mind associated with conscience, morality, and "higher" expectations. Thus the poem can be read as presenting human experience—especially the experience of time— quite realistically. It can be read as offering good, solid, practical advice to enjoy life while enjoyment is still possible. And, in the endorsement of marriage (14), the poem can be seen as speaking for the superego, which seeks to tame, control, and regulate the pleasure principle, bringing it into line with what is "right" and "proper" (such as a lifelong commitment to a person one genuinely loves rather than merely desires). Lacanians might see this poem as reflecting psychological conflict, whereas more conservative

Freudians might see it as a poem in which the three basic aspects of the psyche exist in relative balance and harmony with one another. FEMINIST critics might have interestingly different responses to this poem—a point worth emphasizing, since feminists are often stereotyped in various ways. Some feminists, for instance, might see the poem as a typical instance of male chauvinism, in which women are objectified and are urged to behave in ways intended to give pleasure to males. Particularly interesting to feminists of this sort is the implied warning offered in the final two lines. There the speaker seems to suggest that unless women marry when they are young, they run the risk of becoming "old maids" who are no longer marriageable because they are no longer physically desirable. The implication is that male interest in women is largely physical. These, then, are some of the ways in which some feminists might respond to Herrick's poem.

Other feminists, on the other hand, might see the poem as a welcome endorsement of feminine pleasure, especially feminine sexual pleasure. In Herrick's era (as before and later), a double standard often prevailed: women were often expected to be particularly "virtuous" (more so than men) and actually chaste (except in marriage). Unexpectedly, then, Herrick's poem could have been read in his own day as acknowledging and supporting the right of women to enjoy themselves physically. Admittedly, the poem does suggest that pleasure, for women, should occur within the context of marriage, but at least pleasure for women is something the poem takes seriously and approves. Some feminists, then, might welcome this poem for acknowledging and legitimizing the sensual needs and desires of females.

READER-RESPONSE critics believe that different readers, such as the different kinds of feminists just mentioned, might respond to the very same text in significantly different ways. Some readers, for example, might enjoy this poem's message that the period of youth is a time to enjoy pleasures, while other readers might regard the poem as encouraging self-indulgent irresponsibility. Even the very same reader, at different stages of his or her life, might react to the poem in different ways. Imagine, for instance, a young woman reader who feels strait-jacketed by the demands of her parents, church, and/or society that she be especially "virtuous" sexually by "saving herself" for the right man. Such a reader might either approve or disapprove of the poem's endorsement of feminine sensual pleasure within the context of marriage. On the other hand, imagine that same woman at a later, much older stage in her life. That woman might respond to the poem by regretting social pressures to marry, or by regretting a failure to marry when she had a chance, or by regretting that she failed to enjoy herself when she was young, or by regretting that she placed *too* much emphasis on mere enjoyment during her youth, when her time might have been better spent. In short, it is possible to imagine an enormous variety of responses to this poem, and indeed to any literary text. For reader-response critics, no text is likely to provoke precisely the same response in different readers, and responses can vary greatly even from the same reader during different times, moods, or circumstances.

DIALOGICAL critics might be especially interested in the fact that this poem specifically addresses a particular audience—namely, "Virgins" (i.e., young unmarried women). Using a light, jaunty, humorous tone, the speaker playfully discusses a very serious issue, offering advice in ways that seem designed to make his counsel seem appealing and persuasive. The speaker's voice is relaxed and colloquial (especially when he uses such terms as "a-flying" [2] and "a-getting" [6]), although the final two lines arguably shift to a darker, more ominous tone. Yet the various "voices" implied in Herrick's text are more complicated still, because anyone familiar with classical and/or Renaissance literature cannot help but read this lyric as a *carpe diem* poem and thus as part of a long tradition of similar writings. Such writings were especially popular in Herrick's own day (and Herrick himself was the author of many such pieces). Therefore, merely by writing this text Herrick is engaged in a kind of dialogue with previous writers, with his own contemporaries, and even with himself. By urging virgins to "marry" (14) rather than merely have sex, Herrick adjusts his poem to the Christian sensibilities dominant during his era. Thus, yet another voice enters this dialogue of varying kinds of voices, a dialogue which had already been exceptionally complex even before the reference to marriage arrived. Dialogical critics are especially interested in texts in which various kinds of "voices" can be detected, and although the novel (for that reason) is the genre that most fascinates most of them, even an apparently "simple" lyric poem like this one can seem more complex in its tones than we might at first assume.

14

Katherine Philips (1632–64):

"Upon the Double Murder of King Charles"; "Friendship's Mystery"

Katherine Philips is known today mainly as one of the most influential women poets of her time, especially for her celebrations of female friendship. But she also had strong political opinions and sided with the monarchy during the English civil wars. She was appalled by the eventual beheading of King Charles I on 30 January 1649 and reacted angrily, in the following poem, to the efforts by Vavasour Powell, a radical preacher, to justify the king's execution.

UPON THE DOUBLE MURDER OF KING CHARLES

In Answer to a Libelous Rhyme made by V.P.
I think not on the state, nor am concerned
Which way soever that great helm is turned,
But as that son whose father's danger nigh
Did force his native dumbness, and untie
His fettered organs: so here is a cause   [5]
That will excuse the breach of nature's laws.
Silence were now a sin: nay passion now
Wise men themselves for merit would allow.

What noble eye could see, (and careless pass)
The dying lion kicked by every ass?   [10]
Hath Charles so broke God's laws, he must not have
A quiet crown, nor yet a quiet grave?
Tombs have been sanctuaries; thieves lie here
Secure from all their penalty and fear.
Great Charles his double misery was this,   [15]
Unfaithful friends, ignoble enemies;
Had any heathen been this prince's foe,
He would have wept to see him injured so.
His title was his crime, they'd reason good
To quarrel at the right they had withstood.   [20]
He broke God's laws, and therefore he must die,
And what shall then become of thee and I?
Slander must follow treason; but yet stay,
Take not our reason with our king away.
Though you have seized upon all our defense,   [25]
Yet do not sequester our common sense.
But I admire not at this new supply:
No bounds will hold those who at scepters fly.
Christ will be King, but I ne'er understood,
His subjects built his kingdom up with blood   [30]
(Except their own) or that he would dispense
With his commands, though for his own defense.
Oh! to what height of horror are they come
Who dare pull down a crown, tear up a tomb!

LONGINUS emphasized the need both for writers and, thereby, their writings to be lofty, elevated, inspired, and inspiring. He might therefore be impressed by Philips' poem not only because it commits itself to high ethical standards but also because it condemns others for falling short of such standards. The speaker begins by disavowing any interest in politics per se (1–2). Instead, she claims to be motivated by natural, innate moral instincts— instincts of the sort that might cause a mute son to gain speech suddenly and speak out on behalf of an endangered father (3–5). To remain silent in the face of attacks on King Charles would be sinful; in fact, virtuous passion (of the sort extolled by Longinus) is now (she feels) completely justified (7–8). The speaker presents herself as a spokeswoman for nobility (9, 16), as an opponent of cheap abuse of other persons (10), as a defender of the dead (11–14), as a representative of true friendship (16), and so on. In short, the speaker claims to be inspired by a passionate commitment to what is just, right, and proper, and she presents attackers of the dead king (such as Powell) as low-minded, small, and petty. Longinus would probably admire her enthusiasm both in defending virtue and in condemning vice.

FORMALIST critics, with their strong concern with matters of artistic skill and craftsmanship, might be especially interested in this poem by Philips. After all, political poems are especially likely to be assessed in terms of the ideas they express and the historical contexts they imply. This temptation to discuss them thematically and historically means that their strengths and/or weaknesses *as works of art* tend to be ignored. Formalists, however, would particularly want to understand the aspects of Philips' poem that make it artistically and rhetorically effective. They might note, for instance, the balanced syntax of line 1, the metaphor alluding to the ship of state in line 2, the vivid, well-developed simile of lines 3–5, the almost onomatopoeic effect of "breach" in line 6, and the effective use of double alliteration (emphasizing both "s" and "n" sounds) in line 7. Formalists might also appreciate the striking imagery and word-play on "ass" in line 10, the balanced syntax of line 12, the clever irony of lines 13–14, the effective break at the end of line 15, the balanced syntax of line 16, and the sarcastic irony of lines 17–18.

The brevity of the first half of line 19 is made all the more effective by that half-line's use of assonance, and the irony that immediately ensues (19–20) is also powerful. Particularly effective is the direct address to the reader in line 22, and the poem's memorability is enhanced by the clipped, balanced syntax of lines 23–4 and also by line 24's effective use of assonance and the ironic internal rhyme of "treason" and "reason." Formalists might admire the metaphor implied in line 25 and the word-play on "sequester" in line 26, but they might seek further information about the use of "supply" in line 27 before deciding whether that word "works" as well as another word might have done. The appropriate echo of "k" sounds in the first half of line 29 works well; the use of "understood" in that line looks back to the poem's whole emphasis on the proper use of reason; and the parenthetical phrase in line 31 seems all the more emphatic and effective precisely because it *is* parenthetical.

Finally, the double use of exclamation marks in the last two lines brings the poem to an effectively emphatic conclusion, especially when combined with the alliteration of "height of horror" and the balanced syntax of "pull down" and "tear up" in a poem full of such syntactical equilibrium. Anything that called attention to the poem's effectiveness *as a piece of language* would interest formalists.

Appreciation of Philips' skill and artistry seems especially important because women writers (like other kinds of marginalized authors) have often long been ignored as artists and have sometimes been valued more as token representatives of a group than as genuinely talented writers. Formalists try to pay all authors the artistic respect they deserve.

NEW HISTORICIST critics would focus on the complex historical resonances and contexts (plural) of Philips' poem. They might, for instance, note that it was still relatively unusual, in Philips' day, for a woman even to be literate, let alone take such a strong political stand on paper or in person. Paradoxically, the outbreak of the English civil wars and the partial breakdown of the national Anglican church had helped inspire political outspokenness not only by women like Philips but also by religious radicals such as Vavasour Powell. Also paradoxical is the fact that it is Philips, the woman, who here upholds traditional patriarchal values, whereas it is Powell, the male, who challenges them. Philips in this poem operates as an outspoken woman by defending God and the king, two of the most important male figures in her culture.

New historicists might note that Philips begins by implicitly defending her right and indeed her obligation to speak (1–6). She realizes that to some readers it might seem a "breach of nature's laws" (6) for a woman to be so outspoken on a public issue; therefore she proclaims that it would be sinful to be silent now, thus making her conventional allegiance to God and Christian values the justification of her unconventional behavior. In this sense, there may be a particular political effectiveness in her imagining the approval of "Wise *men*" (italics added) instead of (say) merely "The wise." For new historicists, every aspect of life is inherently political—that is, a matter of possessing or not possessing power. In this poem, Philips not only exercises the kind of literary power that interests formalists but claims and exercises the kind of political power that interests new historicists. She behaves politically not only in the obvious "macropolitical" senses of the word (by focusing on matters of the national religion and national politics) but also in various "micropolitical" senses as well. She asserts her power as an individual, a woman, a wife, a member of her larger family, a member of her local community, etc. None of these aspects of her life, or anyone's life, would seem unimportant to a new historicist seeking to understand the multiple historical and political contexts of Philips' poem.

STRUCTURALIST critics would examine the various "codes" embedded in Philips' poem. Such codes would be multiple and overlapping and would usually involve "binary opposites," with each term helping to define the opposite term with which it is paired. In the opening line, for instance, "Silence" is the opposite of (and therefore paired with) speech; likewise, "sin" is the opposite of (and therefore paired with) virtue. It is impossible to understand the meaning of silence without understanding the meaning of speech, and the same is true of sin and virtue. All codes, for structuralists, are rooted in pairs of opposites. We take most of these codes for granted and do not even especially notice them when reading, but they are crucial (structuralists would argue) to accurate communication and comprehension. Understanding the "code" that is the English language is, for example, crucial to comprehending Philips' poem or any other work written in English.

Other codes or systems of meaning (a structuralist would maintain) are embedded in Philips' poem. Thus the poem is not simply a poem per se but is a satirical poem; it therefore obeys many of the rules associated with the genre of satire. The code that pits reason against passion is also crucial to this text and is already implied in line 1. Knowing all the various codes associated with Christianity can help readers understand this poem, and another code implied here is the code associated with showing respect to the dead. In short, the entire poem—like any text—depends on various codes, and those codes may vary from one culture to another. For instance, we no longer assume, in modern Western culture, that women need to justify themselves when they speak out on contentious political issues, but the first eight lines of Philips' poem seem to suggest that she did, in fact, feel the need to justify her own boldness in writing this poem.

DECONSTRUCTORS, as the word implies, think that the codes studied by structuralists are much messier and less coherent than structuralists assume. In general, they think that human communication is much less simple and straightforward than many other theorists believe. Deconstructors argue that writing in particular is typically open to multiple, often conflicting interpretations. Thus, they might argue that the first two lines of Philips' poem are blatantly self-contradictory: by the very act of writing about Charles and his execution, she is quite obviously thinking about "the state" and expressing opinions about the way the "great helm is turned." She admits that by speaking out she is breaching "nature's laws" (6), but she claims that by doing so she is obeying the commands of other such laws. If one supposed law of nature conflicts with another supposed law of nature (as they often seem to do), then a deconstructor might ask whether such "laws" are really "laws" at all, and how one decides how and by whom they are interpreted? In fact, if they even need interpretation, and if they are subject to conflicting interpretations, then we find ourselves in precisely the situation that most interests deconstructors—a situation in which interpretation seems endless and in which some interpretations can seem irresolvable. For deconstructors, there is no end to interpretation and no escape from it.

FRIENDSHIP'S MYSTERY, TO MY DEAREST LUCASIA

1
Come, my Lucasia, since we see
    That Miracles Men's faith do move,
By wonder and by prodigy
    To the dull angry world let's prove
    There's a Religion in our Love.   [5]

2
For though we were design'd t' agree,
    That Fate no liberty destroys,
But our Election is as free
    As Angels, who with greedy choice
    Are yet determin'd to their joys.   [10]

3
Our hearts are doubled by the loss,
    Here Mixture is Addition grown;

We both diffuse, and both ingross:
  And we whose minds are so much one,
  Never, yet ever are alone.   [15]

4

We court our own Captivity
  Than Thrones more great and innocent:
'Twere banishment to be set free,
  Since we wear fetters whose intent
  Not Bondage is, but Ornament.   [20]

5

Divided joys are tedious found,
  And griefs united easier grow:
We are our selves but by rebound,
  And all our Titles shuffled so,
  Both Princes, and both Subjects too.   [25]

6

Our Hearts are mutual Victims laid,
  While they (such power in Friendship lies)
Are Altars, Priests, and Off'rings made:
  And each Heart which thus kindly dies,
  Grows deathless by the Sacrifice.   [30]

PLATO generally distrusted poetry because he felt that it often expressed and appealed to mere emotion rather than encouraging the use of the higher powers of reason and intelligence. He believed that poetry, in general, had too great an influence in Greek society during his era, and so he celebrated philosophy—the love and development of genuine wisdom—as an alternative. Plato, however, might admire Philips' poem for several reasons. In the first place, the poem extols friendship, a relationship that classical thinkers believed was ideally rooted in mutual love of virtue. Second, this particular poem is highly intellectual in its phrasing, arguments, and methods. It is a perfect example of the intellectually weighty poetry often called "metaphysical" and often associated with the example of John Donne. Rather than offering an outpouring of mere emotion, Philips presents a series of paradoxical arguments that demand that readers *think* about her claims instead of responding reflexively to simple, heart-felt sentiments. Philips avoids mere sentimentality, even when dealing with a subject that could easily have lent itself to sentimental expression.

THEMATIC critics are especially interested in the ideas or concepts literature explores. They would be especially interested in this poem's treatment of the idea (and ideal) of friendship. Friendship—particularly friendship between men—was an especially common motif in Renaissance literature and culture. Already, then, Philips works an important variation on the theme by celebrating friendship between two women. Friendship was such an important ideal during the Renaissance partly because friendship was, ideally, a freely elected relationship. Most other important relationships people experienced during this era were, to one degree or another, rooted in biology (such as the relations between and among parents, children, and siblings) or in social status or economic class. Even marriages were still often heavily influenced by parental approval. Philips' poem, then, celebrates one of the few relationships common in her culture that depended mainly on free individual choice. Indeed, she dwells on this issue of choice explicitly (as in lines 6–10 and 16–20), and her poem reflects many standard assumptions about friendship that were common in her era. These ideas had been developed and explained at great length in many writings of the period—writings that were in turn influenced by classical treatises on the subject, such as Cicero's famous essay *De Amicitia* (On Friendship) and numerous others. Thematic critics would be especially interested in how Philips' poem both reflects and departs from her age's standard ideas about relations between friends. One of the most important of those ideas, for instance, was the belief that true friendship resulted from a mutual love of virtue. Yet friendship treatises of Philips' era almost always assume that the friendships they extol are friendships between men. Philips, in contrast, is one of the earliest and most important celebrants of friendships between women.

ARCHETYPAL critics assume that most human beings are fundamentally alike—that they share the same basic human nature. (This is an assumption they share with most ancient theorists, with many theorists who wrote before the second half of the twentieth century, and with many current Darwinian critics.) Archetypal critics would argue that the desire for friendship is one of the most common of all human wants and needs. They would therefore argue that Philips' poem would interest—and appeal to—most people who have ever lived (or will ever live). Yes, the poem focuses on a particular friendship with a particular woman (whose real name was Anne Owen), but that fact would hardly limit the work's general "relevance" in the eyes of archetypal critics. Friendship, they would argue, may have been an especially important issue during the Renaissance, but archetypal critics would claim that it always has been and always will be an interest very widely shared by practically all people.

DIALOGICAL critics, with their interest in the ways literature involves various kinds of interaction (especially between different persons and between different texts), would find Philips' poem genuinely intriguing. Clearly the poem involves a kind of dialogue between the speaker and Lucasia, but the text itself is also "in dialogue" with many other writings about friendship. These texts were composed not only during Philips' era but also earlier, particularly by various classical philosophers (such as Plato, Cicero, Seneca, and others) who extolled relations between true and virtuous friends. Critics have also noted various echoes in Philips' poem of ideas and phrases from poems by John Donne, so that anyone reading her poem who also knew Donne's might see their works as involved in a complicated dialogue, a textual give-and-take. Often her poem echoes specific phrases from Donne's poetry, and her poetry in turn gave rise to many imitations and responses. She was in fact one of the most widely read women poets of her age and was thus a crucial voice in the cultural dialogue of her time.

MULTICULTURAL critics are especially interested in texts written by, or appealing to, members of various minority groups, whether those groups are racial, ethnic, sexual, etc., or some combination of these communities (or others). Philips' poems, for instance, have often been embraced by lesbian readers, who have seen them as some of the earliest and most eloquent celebrations of same-sex relations among women. Whether or not Philips herself was a practicing lesbian (a matter of some debate), her works easily can be read as expressions of lesbian desire and same-sex love, and it has become increasingly common to read them in just that way. Philips is one of many authors who have benefited from recent interest in writings by homosexuals or writings of interest to homosexual readers. Multiculturalists, like many recent theorists of other sorts, tend to emphasize the distinctiveness of individual persons or groups rather than their similarities. They also tend to be interested in the way literature can either inhibit or help foster progressive social change, by which they mean greater power and freedom for previously marginalized groups or individuals. Multicultural critics might be especially interested in the ways Philips, in this poem, appropriates the language and ideas of standard classical and Christian thinkers to justify close bonds between women—bonds that may even have been lesbian in one sense of another.

15

Andrew Marvell (1621–78):

"To His Coy Mistress"; "The Mower against Gardens"

To His Coy Mistress

Marvell's "To His Coy Mistress" is one of the most famous of all English "*carpe diem*" poems, in which a speaker (usually male) urges someone else (usually female) to "seize the day," often by giving in to the speaker's amorous advances (see Chapters 8 and 13). In Marvell's poem, the speaker argues that because time is limited, he and the woman should have sex sooner rather than later. Some readers sympathize with the speaker and admire his wit; others read the poem as ironic mockery of him.

> Had we but world enough and time,
> This coyness, lady, were no crime.
> We would sit down, and think which way
> To walk, and pass our long love's day.
> Thou by the Indian Ganges' side [5]
> Shouldst rubies find; I by the tide
> Of Humber would complain. I would
> Love you ten years before the flood,
> And you should, if you please, refuse

Till the conversion of the Jews.   [10]
My vegetable love should grow
Vaster than empires and more slow;
An hundred years should go to praise
Thine eyes, and on thy forehead gaze;
Two hundred to adore each breast,   [15]
But thirty thousand to the rest;
An age at least to every part,
And the last age should show your heart.
For, lady, you deserve this state,
Nor would I love at lower rate.   [20]
    But at my back I always hear
Time's wingèd chariot hurrying near;
And yonder all before us lie
Deserts of vast eternity.
Thy beauty shall no more be found;   [25]
Nor, in thy marble vault, shall sound
My echoing song; then worms shall try
That long-preserved virginity,
And your quaint honour turn to dust,
And into ashes all my lust;   [30]
The grave's a fine and private place,
But none, I think, do there embrace.
    Now therefore, while the youthful hue
Sits on thy skin like morning dew,
And while thy willing soul transpires   [35]
At every pore with instant fires,
Now let us sport us while we may,
And now, like amorous birds of prey,
Rather at once our time devour
Than languish in his slow-chapped power.   [40]
Let us roll all our strength and all
Our sweetness up into one ball,
And tear our pleasures with rough strife
Through the iron gates of life:
Thus, though we cannot make our sun   [45]
Stand still, yet we will make him run.

ARISTOTLE admired the skill and craftsmanship required to create
an effective work of literature. He might therefore commend, for

instance, the heavy metrical emphasis on the final three syllables of line 4 of Marvell's poem, as well as the use of alliteration and assonance there. The words "long love's day" actually *sound* long and drawn out, so that their meaning seems reinforced by their real or imagined pronunciation. Aristotle might also admire the effective contrast between the reference to the exotic Ganges River in India and the reference to the much less exciting Humber River in England (5–7). A reinforcing contrast (this one even more extreme) appears in lines 7–10. These lines now emphasize not mere geographical distance but a huge gap in time. Indeed, Aristotle might appreciate how the second half of the opening verse paragraph is unified by its emphasis on time, which is in fact one of the entire work's major themes. The poem thus achieves real but also complex unity of imagery, idea, and argument. Many readers have also admired the tight coherence of the poem's argumentative structure, and Aristotle would probably admire it as well: *if* we had time . . . ; *but* we do not . . .; *therefore* we should have sex. Aristotle would respect all this textual evidence (and much more) indicating Marvell's talent not only in the use of individual words, sounds, and images but also in the ability to make all the elements of the poem cohere.

FORMALIST critics, who are heavily influenced by Aristotle, might praise "To His Coy Mistress" for many of the same reasons just outlined, as well as many others. They might also, however, be especially interested in the claim (made by numerous critics) that the poem should be read ironically. Irony almost always intrigues formalists, and indeed the term "irony" (interpreted in various broad senses) is crucial to much formalist writing. Irony, after all, implies the ability to balance simultaneously at least two different meanings, especially meanings that might seem contradictory. Irony, then, almost by its very nature, appeals to the formalist emphasis on complex unity.

Anyone inclined to interpret this poem ironically can point to much supporting evidence. It might seem ironic, for instance, that the speaker hyperbolically accuses the woman of committing a "crime" (2) by refusing to have sex with him. After all if the woman is unmarried (or married to someone else), it would be the *speaker* who would be proposing metaphorically criminal behavior, at least according to the civil and religious standards of Marvell's era. The frequent use of religious language throughout the poem might seem to reinforce this ironic kind of reading, especially the allusions to the worldwide punishment of sin during the Biblical Flood (8) and also to the Last Judgment at the end of earthly time (10, 18). The speaker's explicit reference to his "lust" (30) can also be read as an ironically candid admission of his own ethical standards, while his continual emphasis on the woman's body (rather than mentioning anything having to do with her character or soul) can additionally seem ironic, especially when he tells her that she deserves the high praise he is offering and that he would not love her at a "lower rate" (20). His assumption that nothing exists beyond the physical world (24); his emphasis on mere physical beauty (25); his obscene pun on the word "quaint" (29, which is the root of the modern word "cunt"); and much, much else can be read ironically by anyone so inclined to react to the poem this way. Formalists might or might not agree with this particular interpretation of Marvell's poem, but they would certainly insist on the method of close reading and on martialing detailed evidence to support any interpretation of this or any other work.

READER-RESPONSE critics assume that different readers tend to respond differently to the very same works. Indeed, they assume that even the very *same* readers may respond differently at different times, in different moods, or under different influences. Particular personal experiences are especially likely to influence distinct reader responses. If we assume, for instance, that the speaker of this poem and the woman he is trying to seduce are unmarried, then personal attitudes toward premarital sex might definitely influence how readers react to the speaker and his arguments (and to the woman as well). Likewise, familiarity (or lack of familiarity) with other *carpe diem* poems might influence how one interprets this work. Persons familiar with the Bible are likely to hear more significance in the poem's biblical allusions than persons less familiar with Christian scriptures, while women and men might also react in different ways to the man and woman presented here. In short, what matters most to reader-response critics are the specific reactions of individual readers (or groups of readers), and such reactions are unpredictable and are likely to be very diverse.

POSTMODERNIST critics share, with reader-response theorists, an emphasis on diversity of possible interpretations. Whereas Aristotelians and formalists often try to find evidence to support a single justifiable interpretation of a given work, postmodernists are like many other recent theorists (including deconstructors) in assuming that single "correct" interpretations are probably impossible and not even especially desirable. Thus the fact that the very same words can be read either straightforwardly or ironically would not surprise postmodernists, who doubt that truth is even possible, especially in interpretations of literature. This poem seems to pose interpretive problems (for instance: how could a presumably Christian writer such as Marvell write a poem that seems to champion premarital sex?), but such difficulties are precisely what postmodernists would expect in almost any situation requiring interpretation. Rather than attempting to impose or force a single "correct" meaning on the poem, postmodernists would expect (and even welcome) its openness to different, even contradictory readings.

DARWINIAN critics tend to assume that most males of most species have an innate tendency to seek sex as often and as widely as possible. After all, over many generations the males who passed on the most copies of their genes have been males who have impregnated as many females as they could. Males (most Darwinians believe) face little risk and reap great biological advantages by producing as many offspring as they can. Females, on the other hand, have until recently (before the advent of effective birth control) had every reason to be very selective in choosing their sexual partners. Females of various species have therefore tended to seek partners who were not only strong, healthy, and attractive but also willing to make long-term commitments to supporting the women with whom they mated and the offspring who resulted. It would not surprise Darwinians in the least that so much literature (including Marvell's poem) depicts sexually eager men trying to persuade sexually cautious women into having sex with them.

THE MOWER AGAINST GARDENS

Luxurious man, to bring his vice in use,
    Did after him the world seduce,
And from the fields the flowers and plants allure,
    Where nature was most plain and pure.
He first enclosed within the gardens square   [5]
    A dead and standing pool of air,
And a more luscious earth for them did knead,

Which stupified them while it fed.
The pink grew then as double as his mind;
The nutriment did change the kind.   [10]
With strange perfumes he did the roses taint,
And flowers themselves were taught to paint.
The tulip, white, did for complexion seek,
And learned to interline its cheek:
Its onion root they then so high did hold,   [15]
That one was for a meadow sold.
Another world was searched, through oceans new,
To find the Marvel of Peru.
And yet these rarities might be allowed
To man, that sovereign thing and proud,   [20]
Had he not dealt between the bark and tree,
Forbidden mixtures there to see.
No plant now knew the stock from which it came;
He grafts upon the wild the tame:
That th' uncertain and adulterate fruit   [25]
Might put the palate in dispute.
His green seraglio has its eunuchs too,
Lest any tyrant him outdo.
And in the cherry he does nature vex,
To procreate without a sex.   [30]
'Tis all enforced, the fountain and the grot,
While the sweet fields do lie forgot:
Where willing nature does to all dispense
A wild and fragrant innocence:
And fauns and fairies do the meadows till,   [35]
More by their presence than their skill.
Their statues, polished by some ancient hand,
May to adorn the gardens stand:
But howsoe'er the figures do excel,
The gods themselves with us do dwell.   [40]

PLATO might admire this poem for various reasons. First, it develops a consistent argument, suggesting that unadulterated nature is superior to anything artificial. Because Plato believed that literature should teach valuable philosophical lessons and should appeal to reason and logic rather than emotion and passions, he might commend the argumentative, philosophical aspects of this text. The Mower uses one example after another to illustrate his basic comparisons of nature with virtue and of artifice with vice. Plato would especially applaud the poem's emphasis on morality; for him, one of the chief functions of literature (to the extent that he valued literature at all) was to encourage people to embrace the good, reject the bad, and promote ethical thought and behavior both in individuals and in society at large. Marvell's poem draws on traditional Christian teachings to associate artificiality with superficiality. It also links artificiality with worldly, emotional, material, mutable distractions as opposed to immaterial, spiritual, immutable values. Some analysts even see the poem as an implied endorsement of seventeenth-century Puritanism, with its emphasis on plainness and simplicity, as opposed to the more elaborate, more "showy" (from a Puritan viewpoint) kind of Christianity associated with the Anglican and Roman Catholic churches.

TRADITIONAL HISTORICAL critics might be especially interested in exploring the possibility that the poem is relevant to the conflict between Puritans and other kinds of Christians. They would particularly look for any external evidence that might either confirm that interpretation or cast doubt upon it. Ideally they would want to know when, precisely, the poem was written; what, exactly, were Marvell's religious views at the time the poem was composed; how the poem may have been interpreted by contemporary Puritans and their opponents; which earlier texts the poem may allude or respond to; and so on. In short, they would be interested in much of the information reported in the best annotated editions of the poem, such as the ones prepared by Terence Dawson and Robert Scott Dupree and especially the annotated edition of all Marvell's poetry prepared by Nigel Smith. Traditional historical critics would search archives for any hard, solid evidence that might contribute to a fuller understanding of the poem in its particular historical contexts. There would be no predictable, unalterable interpretation of the poem from an historical point of view. Instead, the way the poem would be interpreted would depend greatly on the nature of the historical evidence available, and new or further evidence might always turn up that could significantly affect the ways the poem was read and understood. In particular, discovery of an interpretation of the poem from the pen of Marvell himself would be of enormous interest to historical critics.

MULTICULTURAL critics might argue that this poem, almost by definition, reflects the existence of different cultures (and of cultural conflict) current during Marvell's era. After all, the Mower is making a sustained argument *against* a cultural preference for elaborate, artificial, well-designed gardens. Such gardens were increasingly popular and prevalent in Marvell's time, especially among the wealthy. Therefore this poem can be read as expressing a strong preference for one kind of culture as opposed to another. The possibility that the poem may reflect a conflict between different religious cultures has already been mentioned, and the reference to tulips (13–16) alludes to the so-called tulip craze or tulip mania of the 1630s, in which the prices paid for tulip bulbs rose to preposterous heights before the market suddenly crashed. This "tulip mania" has thus become synonymous with rampant market speculation of any kind, so that implicitly the Mower is satirizing not only a cultural obsession with elaborate gardens but also a cultural obsession with materialism of all sorts. Nigel Smith, in his superb edition of Marvell's poems, notes that the poem reflects disdain for a fanaticism about gardens (*furor hortensis*) that had become increasingly widespread in Marvell's era. This enthusiasm for elaborate, artificial gardens was sometimes seen as a foreign import that was part of a more general corruption of native English culture by international influences, especially from the Continent. Thus Marvell's poem, which might merely seem to deal with plants and flowers, can in some ways be seen as reflecting underlying conflicts between cultures, including conflicts between different classes, different nations, and different kinds of Christianity.

POSTMODERN critics might find themselves feeling far more sympathetic than Marvell's Mower to the kind of intermixing and hybridization the Mower attacks. Postmodernists, after all, reject rigid distinctions between "high" art and "low" art or between "elite" culture and "popular" culture. They often actively advocate the mixing or juxtaposition of diverse styles, genres, motifs, and methods—a fact that makes postmodern architecture some of the most interesting (although some might say "chaotic") that has ever been created. All one need do is look at a building designed, for instance, by Frank Gehry to see the kinds of traits that excite some people about postmodernism and that frustrate others. Postmodernists might enjoy the different sorts of exotic species and unusual designs present in the gardens the Mower attacks, but they might be suspicious and critical of such gardens if those gardens were too rigidly, classically, and symmetrically designed.

Anything that smacked of too much order, predictability, and simplicity would hold little interest for postmodernists. This very poem, for instance, with its mostly regular meter, its strictly regular rhyme scheme, and its predictably alternating line lengths, is not a particularly postmodern work of art. (For a better example of the sort of poetic structure—or nonstructure—a postmodernist might favor, see George Herbert's "The Collar" [Chapter 12].)

ECOCRITICS would be especially intrigued by "The Mower against Gardens." After all, this poem deals explicitly with one of the key interests of ecocriticism: the relationships and interactions between humans and physical nature. On the one hand, ecocritics might admire the gardeners whom the Mower attacks, who take such a strong interest in cultivating nature in practically every sense of that verb. They not only care for species of plants already present but also create new kinds of plants through breeding and grafting. In the process, however, they interfere with nature as it "naturally" exists, and by the very act of establishing elaborate gardens they almost certainly and quite literally uproot plants that had already been growing naturally. They interfere with nature in all sorts of ways that might be perceived as destructive, especially by destroying the habitats of creatures that previously lived among, and fed on, the uncultivated plants. Marvell's mower whimsically claims that "fauns and fairies" once tilled the meadows undisturbed by human gardeners with their elaborate, artificial designs (35). Ecocritics, however, might note that the real residents of those meadows might actually have been such real creatures as fawns and free-growing berries. Even in attempting to cultivate nature, then, humans often destroy and/or restrict it in ways that would disturb ecocritics at least as much as those ways disturb Marvell's Mower. His job of mowing (cutting grass with a scythe) also destroys nature, but not in any permanent way. In a sense, by cutting grass and making hay, the Mower lives in the kind of harmony with nature that ecocritics typically celebrate.

16

John Milton (1608–74):

"Lycidas" (excerpt); *Paradise Lost*, Book 12 (excerpt)

"Lycidas" is one of the most famous and influential of all "pastoral elegies" ever written in English. In it, Milton mourns the death of Edward King, a fellow Cambridge undergraduate who had drowned at sea. Yet Milton also uses the poem to meditate on the meaning and purposes of life (his own in particular) and to satirize what he considered the corruption of the Anglican church of the 1630s. In this opening section, the speaker uses many standard images and motifs of pastoral literature to express his grief over King's premature death.

LYCIDAS (excerpt)

  Yet once more, O ye laurels, and once more
Ye myrtles brown, with ivy never sere,
I come to pluck your berries harsh and crude,
And with forc'd fingers rude
Shatter your leaves before the mellowing year.   [5]
Bitter constraint and sad occasion dear
Compels me to disturb your season due;

For Lycidas is dead, dead ere his prime,
Young Lycidas, and hath not left his peer.
Who would not sing for Lycidas? he knew   [10]
Himself to sing, and build the lofty rhyme.
He must not float upon his wat'ry bier
Unwept, and welter to the parching wind,
Without the meed of some melodious tear.

    Begin then, Sisters of the sacred well   [15]
That from beneath the seat of Jove doth spring;
Begin, and somewhat loudly sweep the string.
Hence with denial vain and coy excuse!
So may some gentle muse
With lucky words favour my destin'd urn,   [20]
And as he passes turn
And bid fair peace be to my sable shroud!

    For we were nurs'd upon the self-same hill,
Fed the same flock, by fountain, shade, and rill;
Together both, ere the high lawns appear'd   [25]
Under the opening eyelids of the morn,
We drove afield, and both together heard
What time the gray-fly winds her sultry horn,
Batt'ning our flocks with the fresh dews of night,
Oft till the star that rose at ev'ning bright   [30]
Toward heav'n's descent had slop'd his westering wheel.
Meanwhile the rural ditties were not mute,
Temper'd to th'oaten flute;
Rough Satyrs danc'd, and Fauns with clov'n heel,
From the glad sound would not be absent long;   [35]
And old Damætas lov'd to hear our song.

    But O the heavy change now thou art gone,
Now thou art gone, and never must return!
Thee, Shepherd, thee the woods and desert caves,
With wild thyme and the gadding vine o'ergrown,   [40]
And all their echoes mourn.
The willows and the hazel copses green
Shall now no more be seen
Fanning their joyous leaves to thy soft lays.

As killing as the canker to the rose,   [45]
Or taint-worm to the weanling herds that graze,
Or frost to flowers that their gay wardrobe wear
When first the white thorn blows:
Such, Lycidas, thy loss to shepherd's ear.

HORACE was (along with Aristotle) one of the two most influential theorists of literature for English Renaissance writers. He would have found much to admire in Milton's poem, particularly because it is such a splendid example of the genre of pastoral elegy, and issues of genre were always important to Horace. Pastoral elegies had been created not only by ancient Greek and Roman poets but also by more recent Renaissance writers, not only on the continent but also in England. Milton draws on all these traditions, thereby managing to satisfy various expectations and preferences of his audience (who were the most important judges of poetry, as far as Horace was concerned). Yet Milton not only "Englishes" a classical kind of writing but also blends a pagan classical poetic form with current Christian ideas, once again suiting his work and theme to the nature of his own audience. He innovates, but he does so within the broad confines of a familiar genre. He depicts various *kinds* of characters (such as young men and an old man), and he depicts them exactly as his readers might have expected them to be presented. He uses his poem both to please and to instruct, and in these and many other ways he writes precisely as Horace had advised, creating a poem that might appeal both to the young and to the old and both to fellow Christians as well as to those familiar with classical and European literary precedents. His phrasing is clear and dignified but is also inventive, especially in the ways it playfully describes Cambridge undergraduates as if they were fellow shepherds. Horace might have worried about the controversial phrasing that enters the poem later, when Milton begins satirizing corrupt Christians, but satire itself was a genre Horace both admired and practiced. Therefore, in this respect as in so many others, Milton had strong classical precedent to justify practically every aspect of his poem. Horace advised poets to follow custom, and Milton does just that.

PSYCHOANALYTIC critics might argue that fear of death (especially premature death) is one of the most widespread of all human fears. It can therefore evoke responses from all three aspects of the human psyche: the emotional id, the rational ego, and the ethical superego. Milton's poetic response to King's early death arguably shows him trying to deal rationally and responsibly with an event that seems to have unsettled him. Later in the poem, in portions not reprinted here, he clearly wonders whether it might be better, as a young man, simply to enjoy the pleasures of life rather than behaving responsibly and submitting himself to various kinds of self-imposed discipline. In other words, he wonders whether it might be best simply to give vent to the impulses of the id rather than obeying strictures originating in the ego and superego. Ultimately he decides, of course, to continue living a life of responsible dedication to lofty ideals, and he condemns those who indulge in the pleasures of the id rather than obligating themselves to God. Even in the lines excerpted here, various aspects of the psyche can be discerned. Thus the emotional id arguably motivates lines 6 and 37–8; the rational, realistic ego arguably motivates lines 18 and 20; and the moral, ethical superego arguably motivates lines 12–14. By the end of the poem, the emotions associated with the id have been expressed but have also been tamed and disciplined by the ego and supergo.

ARCHETYPAL critics would argue that Milton's poem deals with many issues (and expresses many emotions and ideas) that have probably everywhere and always concerned human beings, and that probably always will. The mere fact that pastoral elegies have been written for millennia and that people nearly everywhere and in practically all times have mourned (and still mourn) the dead suggests that Milton is here dealing with archetypal themes and emotions. The deaths of young people have long seemed, practically at all times and in all places, especially unfortunate, and Milton deftly plays on this sense of tragic waste. Similarly, the deaths of other persons has probably nearly always and everywhere inspired thoughts of one's own inevitable mortality, so that once again Milton is dealing in this poem with very fundamental human concerns—concerns that transcend any differences of class, race, gender, nationality, culture, or sexual orientation (to mention just a few of the issues and identities that preoccupy other kinds of critics). The opening lines of the excerpt suggest that Milton has already written poems of mourning and imply that he will probably need to do so again. Death, after all, is one of the crucial facts of human life, and the problem of living a satisfying life is one unconfined to any particular culture, time, or place.

DIALOGICAL critics, with their interest in the various tones and voices a single text might articulate, would be especially interested in Milton's poem. They might also be interested in the various audiences the poem addresses. Clearly the poem would have been read by King's relatives and friends, but it would also have been read by other undergraduates (and probably also teachers) at Cambridge and perhaps by a wider readership, especially in London. Yet Milton is also addressing both himself and his satirical targets, and he is pretty obviously also writing with posterity in mind. The fact that the text has all these different probable addressees inevitably contributes to the poem's complexity.

The poem is also, of course, in a kind of dialogue with the most famous earlier examples of the pastoral elegy, including poems by Theocritus, Moschus, Virgil, various continental poets, and Edmund Spenser and others in England. The Bible, it goes without saying, is another key source of allusions for Milton here, as it is in much of his poetry. Many of his readers would themselves have been familiar not only with the Bible (and with conflicting interpretations of Christian scriptures) but also with many of the classical and Renaissance texts with which *Lycidas* is in dialogue. These readers could be expected to know, for instance, the significance of the references to "laurels" (associated with poetry [1]) and "myrtles" (associated with love [2]), and they would have understood that the decision to call Edward King "Lycidas" was part of a long tradition of using classical names in Renaissance poetry. A few readers may even have heard an echo of the early pastoral elegy titled *Idyll 7*, by Theocritus, where the name "Lycidas" is used in a poem that is itself partly about poetry. In short, dialogical critics would be fascinated by every aspect of the poem's engagement with other texts and diverse readers.

ECOCRITICS would be interested in the mere fact that Milton chose to write a *pastoral* elegy. That decision almost by definition dictated that much of the poem would feature imagery of physical nature, as indeed it does from start to finish. *Lycidas* celebrates the beauty of the natural landscape even as it suggests that life in heaven is superior to existence on earth. By fancifully depicting himself and King as shepherds, Milton reminds us of the obligations of humans to care for and tend to other creatures. This imagery becomes especially resonant when he later uses pastoral imagery to suggest the proper role of right-minded pastors to care for their metaphorical flocks. Milton's poem reminds us of times when most people lived close to the land and were familiar with the work involved in raising crops and tending to animals of all sorts. Of course, Milton does not entirely sentimentalize nature: he reminds us that King died when a storm sank his ship, and he also acknowledges that sheep have natural enemies, including wolves, and that plants can be destroyed by "canker" (45). All in all, Milton uses imagery of nature in ways that would probably please ecocritics, as it has pleased and impressed many other kinds of readers.

Paradise Lost, Book 12 (excerpt)

In the following excerpt, which comes from near the very end of Milton's great epic poem, the archangel Michael has just given Adam a panoramic overview of what will happen in human history now that Adam and Eve have sinned, thereby causing their own fall and the fall of all their descendants.

[Michael] ended; and thus Adam last replied.
How soon hath thy prediction, Seer blest,
Measured this transient world, the race of time,
Till time stand fixed! Beyond is all abyss,   [555]
Eternity, whose end no eye can reach.
Greatly-instructed I shall hence depart;
Greatly in peace of thought; and have my fill
Of knowledge, what this vessel can contain;
Beyond which was my folly to aspire.   [560]
Henceforth I learn, that to obey is best,
And love with fear the only God; to walk
As in his presence; ever to observe
His providence; and on him sole depend,
Merciful over all his works, with good   [565]
Still overcoming evil, and by small
Accomplishing great things, by things deemed weak
Subverting worldly strong, and worldly wise
By simply meek: that suffering for truth's sake
Is fortitude to highest victory,   [570]

And, to the faithful, death the gate of life;
Taught this by his example, whom I now
Acknowledge my Redeemer ever blest.
To whom thus also the Angel last replied.
This having learned, thou hast attained the sum   [575]
Of wisdom; hope no higher, though all the stars
Thou knewest by name, and all the ethereal powers,
All secrets of the deep, all Nature's works,
Or works of God in Heaven, air, earth, or sea,
And all the riches of this world enjoyedst,   [580]
And all the rule, one empire; only add
Deeds to thy knowledge answerable; add faith,
Add virtue, patience, temperance; add love,
By name to come called charity, the soul
Of all the rest: then wilt thou not be loath   [585]
To leave this Paradise, but shalt possess
A Paradise within thee, happier far.

LONGINUS would almost certainly have admired this passage. It exemplifies much that he most valued about the literature he considered "sublime" (i.e., elevated and elevating). The views and ideals expressed here that would have appealed to Longinus include the following: (a) the idea that the physical world and mere materialism are ephemeral and "transient" (554); (b) the idea that one important function of literature is to instruct readers and inspire them to pursue lofty goals (557); (c) the idea that "virtue" is an especially crucial and worthy achievement; and (d) the idea that true happiness resides in the mind and soul and does not result from worldly prosperity (587). Milton and Longinus both believed that only a truly good person could produce valuable literature because much of the value of literature resided in its ability to express and inspire goodness. Adam feels ennobled and enlightened by Michael's instruction, but most of all he feels determined to try to live a better life thanks to Michael's uplifting teachings. Ideally Milton's own readers should feel similarly uplifted by this passage and should emerge from the whole experience of reading *Paradise Lost* feeling "Greatly-instructed" (557) in all the various senses of "Greatly."

  THEMATIC critics, with their emphasis on the key ideas or central motifs of literary works, would be especially interested in this passage from *Paradise Lost*. After all, in this passage Milton spells out quite explicitly some of the crucial concepts that underlay not only his own thinking but also the larger meanings of his poem. This passage exemplifies how important ideas are not only to *Paradise Lost* in general but to Book 12 in particular, especially the concluding section of that book. Milton quite literally spells out the lessons he wants his readers to take away from his epic. Both Adam and Michael articulate as clearly as possible the ideas Milton wants to emphasize. Therefore a passage like this would be especially important to anyone wanting to examine the overall meaning or underlying themes of *Paradise Lost*, and indeed many authors besides Milton have often used the conclusions of their works—particularly long works—as places where lessons, morals, and crucial ideas can be very memorably emphasized. One has only to think of the conclusions of such works as *Beowulf, Sir Gawain and the Green Knight, Hamlet, Othello,* or any of thousands of other important texts to realize that authors often save their most explicit pronouncements for the closing sections of their texts. *Paradise Lost* is a poem in which themes and ideas are unusually important, and so it is not surprising that this poem concludes by stressing the instruction Milton wanted to impart.

FORMALIST critics would readily agree with thematic critics and with Longinus that ideas are very important in this passage, which is one of the most openly didactic portions of the entire poem. Formalists would emphasize, however, that any ideas would have little visceral impact if they were not effectively and memorably expressed. Formalists might argue that even (or perhaps especially) when an author is most intent on teaching, s/he needs to write in artistically skillful and powerful ways. Formalists might note, for instance, the emphatic, monosyllabic conclusion of Adam's opening sentence here, where the abrupt brevity of the phrasing ("Till time stand fixt") seems appropriate to the forcefulness of the statement. Formalists might also note the way Milton unifies his phrasing by emphasizing words or phrases associated with vision, such as "Seer blest" (553), "whose end no eye can reach" (556), and even the word-play on "providence" (564), a term which literally implies (through its Latin roots) the idea of God's foresight. In line 555 as so often elsewhere, Milton skillfully uses alliteration and other sound effects, just as he skillfully uses assonance in line 556. Here as so often elsewhere, he shows his command not only of the meanings of English words but of their sounds as well. Partly because he was blind, Milton had one of the best "ears" of all English poets, and it is not surprising that his poetry is often compared to music in its subtle, memorable effects. This passage also displays Milton's skillful use of such various devices as anaphora (557–8), paradox (562), punning (564), metaphor (571), and especially listing and repetition (565–9, 575–85). Indeed, the second half of the passage, in particular, develops a kind of intoxicating chant-like rhythm that is nearly irresistible simply as a piece of verbal music, no matter what the words actually *mean*. It is easy to imagine someone with no knowledge of English listening to this passage being recited aloud and realizing that *something* important and emphatic is being said here. The cumulative effect of all the listing ("add faith, / Add virtue, patience, temperance; add love . . ." [582–3]) is almost overwhelming, so that even if one has no interest at all in Milton's theology one cannot help but admire his talent for combining words. For formalists, what matters most about *Paradise Lost* is not its message but its artistry. Without Milton's skill as a writer, the poem would be simply another one of the many pieces of religious propaganda written during a period brimming with such works, most of them almost indistinguishable from one another and not especially distinguished in their phrasing.

MARXIST critics might see this passage as in fact essentially a piece of religious propaganda whose effect might be to encourage quiescence, obedience, political passivity, and economic subservience in Milton's readers. Adam's willingness to accept instruction so humbly from Michael might disturb Marxists, especially when he says he is now content to have his "fill / Of knowledge, what this vessel can contain; / Beyond which was [his] folly to aspire" (558–60). This willingness to rest content with religious teachings, this abdication of any desire to learn more than religion can teach, might perfectly illustrate, to many Marxists, the idea that religion is an opiate that seduces people into a kind of unquestioning political stupor. Particularly unsettling, from a Marxist viewpoint, is Adam's proclamation that "to obey is best, / And love with fear the only God; to walk / As in his presence; ever to observe /His providence; and on him sole depend" (561–4). Milton himself, of course, had spent much of his life questioning the powerful, disobeying them, and even justifying the execution of King Charles I, the most powerful secular and religious leader in the land, who was head of both the national government and the national church. Milton had himself been a revolutionary, and he still inspires revolutionary fervor in some of his readers. In the present passage, however, he seems to give aid and comfort to the enemies of revolution. His actual intention in writing these words may have been far more complex than some Marxists might assume: much of his career suggests that he thought the best way to obey God was to disobey worldly authority. But it is easy to see how the passage could be embraced and endorsed by political, social, and economic conservatives to support their own agendas.

NEW HISTORICIST critics might be particularly interested in the historical complications this passage reflects and implies. These complications would be all the more interesting since the passage seems to present simple, clear, unambiguous Christian teachings—the sort of teachings that might lead novice readers to assume there was broad agreement among Christians of Milton's day about the central tenets and implications of their faith. Yet such agreement, of course, was anything but typical of his era, and whereas traditional historical critics might tend to see Milton as simply a great "Christian" poet, new historicists would tend to emphasize the enormous variety of Christians and Christianities that were competing with each other throughout Milton's life. Milton was heavily involved in intra-Christian conflicts. He felt contempt for Roman Catholicism and was almost as contemptuous of the established Church of England. He had served many of the best years of his life as a member of the revolutionary government that had overthrown and abolished the English monarchy, and enormous numbers of his writings are essentially pieces of political and religious propaganda. Milton's whole career illustrates the essential new historicist claim that political conflicts and negotiations are crucial to culture and individual lives at practically every level and in practically every way. There never was (according to new historicists) a time of cultural unanimity and concord. Power struggles, as *Paradise Lost* clearly suggests, have been with us since the beginning of human life on earth and even before, even in heaven, if one assumes that heaven even exists. It is all well and good (a new historicist might say) for Milton to extol love ("by name to come called charity") as the "soul / Of all the rest" of human virtues (583–5), and it may sound beautiful to hear him say that. But for new historicists, conflict is "always already" present in any culture. For them, paradise was never quite lost because it never really existed, at least if we associate paradise with concord and the absence of disagreement and struggle. Milton himself, during the course of his eventful life, went from being relatively powerless to relatively powerful to relatively powerless again, and practically every aspect of his life exemplifies the basic new historicist insight that cultures are sites of struggle at practically every level and in practically every way.

AFTERWORD
CRITICAL PLURALISM: "A CONTEMPLATION ON BASSETS-DOWN-HILL" BY ANNE KEMP

Of all the critical theories described and discussed in this book, which is the best? Which theory is most useful, most relevant, most convincing? To critical pluralists, such questions make little sense. Asking such questions is like asking which tool is best: a screwdriver, a hammer, or a saw? Critical pluralists would argue that each tool is best for a particular purpose: a screwdriver is best for inserting or removing a screw; a hammer is best for driving in or removing a nail; and a saw is best for cutting something one could not easily cut with a knife. Similarly, glasses are best for improving everyday vision; microscopes are best for seeing things that are very small; and telescopes are best for seeing anything extremely far away. X-ray machines have their purposes, and so do MRIs. Similarly, each of the critical theories discussed in this book (and others besides) has its own particular, potential usefulness depending on the kind of critical work a reader or critic wants to accomplish. The best readers and critics are likely to be those whose toolboxes are most full and who know how to use as many tools as competently as possible.

One way to illustrate the attractions and usefulness of pluralism is to use it to explicate a poem that has heretofore been almost totally unknown—a poem not yet widely studied from any particular point of view and that therefore seems especially open to many. One such poem is the following, which has only recently begun to receive any attention. It was originally printed as a "broadside" leaflet around 1658:

> A Contemplation on //Bassets-down-
> Hill by the most Sacred adorer
> of the Muses Mr^s. A.K.

//Neare Meysey=
Ha[m]pton or Down=
Ampney in Gloust-
ershire [this is a manuscript note to left of printed title; "Anne Kemp" is written in ink to the right of the printed initials]

If that exact Apelles now did live. [sic]
  And would a picture of Elizium give;
He might pourtrai'ct the prospect which this Hill
Doth shew; & make the eie command at will.
Heer's many a shire whose pleasauntness for sight   [5]
Doth yeild to the Spectators great delight.
Ther's a large Feild guilded with Ceres gold;
Here a green mead doth many Heifers hold: [sic]
Ther's pasture growne with virdant grass, whose store,
Of Argent-sheep shewes th'owner is not poore.   [10]
Here springs doe intricate Meanders make
Excelling farr Oblivion's Lethe Lake.
There woods and Coppises harbour as many
And sweet melodious Choristers, as any
Elizium yeilds; whose Philomel'an laies   [15]
Merit the highest of the Lyrick's praise.
Heer's Flora deck't with robes of Or, and Azur,
Fragrently smelling yeild's two senses pleasure.
Hence Zephirus doth breath his gentle gales
Coole on the Hills, and sweet throughout the Vales
[sic: no punc]   [20]
How happy are they that in this Climate dwell?
Alas! They can't their owne sweet welfare tell;
Scarce I my selfe whil'st I am here doe know it
Till I see it's Antithesis to shew it.
Here are no smoaking streets, nor howling cryes,   [25]
Deafening the eares, nor blinding of the eyes;
No noysome smells t'infect, and choacke the aire,

Breeding diseases envious to the Faire.
Deceipt is here exil'd from Flesh, and Bloud:
(Strife only reigns, for all strive to be good.)   [30]
    With Will his verse I here will make an end
    And as the Crab doth alwaies backward bend
    So, though from this sweet place I goe away
    My loyall heart will in this Climate stay.
        Thus heartles, doth my worthless body rest [35]
        Whilest my heart liveth ever with the [*sic*] ever
        blest.

What are we to make of this poem? Who was Anne Kemp? What does the poem "mean," and does it succeed as a work of art? In what various ways might the poem be studied? Pluralists would suggest that there are *many* possible answers to such questions.

    Probably it is most useful to begin by paraphrasing the poem, so that we understand as clearly as possible what it is actually saying.

Prose paraphrase

Title and note: The muses are the classical goddesses of poetry and various other arts and kinds of knowledge. Almost nothing is known about Anne Kemp, if she was indeed the author of this poem. Apparently Bassets Downhill was an elevated area near the Gloucester villages of Meysey-Hampton and Down Ampney, which still exist.

Lines 1–6: Apelles was a great classical Greek artist, known for the astonishingly realistic precision (or "exact[ness]") of his paintings. If "exact Apelles" were living now, when I am writing this poem, and if he wanted to draw or paint Elysium (the abode of the blessed, which resembles paradise), he might depict the view from the hill where I am now standing. He could, by creating such a painting, control the eyes of any viewers. Spectators can greatly delight in the views of all the shires (or counties) they can see from this hill.

Lines 7–10: Over there is a large field gilded with the yellow color of grains. Grains are associated with Ceres, the ancient goddess of fertility (from whose name the word "cereal" derives). Here a green meadow holds many heifers. (Heifers are young cows that have not yet given birth to calves.) Over there is a pasture filled with green (or "verdant") grass; that other pasture contains a "store" (or large quantity) of silver- (or "argent") colored sheep. Their presence shows that the person who owns the pasture is not poor.

Lines 11–12: In this other place visible from the hill, springs make complicated, meandering motions; they surpass the lake created by the famous Lethe river, one of the rivers in Hades (the underworld). (The dead are obliged to taste the waters of Lethe so that they may forget everything they did or said when they were alive; hence Lethe is often associated with forgetfulness.)

Lines 13–16: Over there, in another area, woods and thickets of small trees ("copses") are the homes to as many and sweet singing birds as any that can be found in Elysium. The songs of these birds, which resemble the songs of nightingales ("Philomel'an lays"), deserve the highest praise that lyric poetry can bestow.

Lines 17–20: Over here is Flora, the Roman goddess of flowers, dressed in robes of gold ("or") and blue ("azur" or "azure"). These flowers smell so good and look so beautiful that they please both the nose and the eyes. From this place ("hence"), Zephyrus (or Zephyr), the god of the western wind, blows his gentle breezes; they are cool on the hills and sweet throughout the valleys.

Lines 21–4: How happy are the people who dwell in this climate! (Note: people in the seventeenth century sometimes used exclamation marks where we would use question marks.) Alas! They can't tell how fortunate their conditions are. Even I myself, while I am here in this beautiful place, don't really know how wonderful this place is until I see its opposite. Seeing a different kind of place helps me appreciate the place where I am now standing.

Lines 25–30: Here, in this place (unlike in a huge city such as London) are no smoking streets or howling cries that deafen the ears or blind the eyes. Here, unlike in a huge city, there are no annoying smells that infect and choke the air, breeding diseases (such as smallpox) that hate human beauty. There is no deceit here in the beautiful countryside (although there is in huge cities). The only kind of strife that reigns here in the country is the strife to be good.

Lines 31–6: I will now echo the poet Will Shakespeare, who had Ophelia promise in *Hamlet* to "make an end on't" (i.e., "on it"). I will also echo Shakespeare another time by alluding to Hamlet's snide remark to Polonius: "yourself, sir, shall grow old as I am—if like a crab you could go backward." Just as the crab walks backward, so, even though I have to leave this beautiful place, my heart will stay here. Therefore, my worthless body now lacks a heart because my heart lives always with you ("with the[e]") ever blessed.

Notice how much of this paraphrase depends on providing solid historical information, especially in identifying allusions to particular figures or texts. Once the "plain" meaning of the text is paraphrased, however, we are better-positioned to look at the poem from varied points of view—in other words, to examine it pluralistically. Pluralists would argue that one of the best ways to understand this poem or any literary work is to explore it in as many ways as possible, using the diverse perspectives already outlined in this book as well as others.

PLATO, who emphasized the need for morality in literature and society, might especially appreciate lines 29–30. They, after all, condemn deceit and praise virtue, paradoxically asserting that the only strife near Bassets Downhill is competition to be good. The whole point of Kemp's text, from a Platonic point of view, is to celebrate external rural beauty and associate it with the internal beauty of virtue.

ARISTOTLE extolled careful literary craftsmanship, especially evidence of complexity and coherence. He might therefore appreciate how Kemp begins by alluding to one of the greatest visual artists of Western history—Apelles—as well as how she ends by alluding to one of the greatest English dramatists (Shakespeare). These bookended references to two different kinds of art and artists give the work a symmetry that matches its additionally symmetrical emphasis on the country and the city.

HORACE admired poetry that was realistic, clearly written, well designed, and likely to appeal to many kinds of readers. He would therefore probably admire Kemp's lyric, which realistically depicts both the countryside and the city. Her lucid descriptions might appeal both to lovers of the countryside and to city dwellers who longed for a simpler, cleaner, healthier place to live. Many residents of the cities of Kemp's time would have recently immigrated from rural areas, and so her poem might especially appeal both to people still living in the country and to readers who had recently moved from there.

LONGINUS thought literature should both reflect, and appeal to, the highest, noblest aspects of human nature. Like Plato, he would almost certainly value the way Kemp rejects deceit and praises virtue, especially her idea that people should compete to be good rather than wealthy. Kemp celebrates both the beauty of nature and the beauty of lives lived in tune with nature. Longinus, who thought the best literature was the most inspiring, might therefore have valued Kemp's text.

TRADITIONAL HISTORICAL critics would attempt to provide as much factual information as possible about this poem. In particular, they would want to know whether Kemp was indeed the author and, if so, who she was, where she lived, why she wrote, what else (if anything) she may have written, and anything else about her. They might be especially intrigued by her references not only to Shakespeare but to *Hamlet*. She alludes to both as if both were well known.

THEMATIC critics, who emphasize the key ideas in literary works, would almost certainly focus on how Kemp treats the themes of country versus city, nature versus artifice, and simplicity versus complexity. They might read the poem as suggesting either that country life is better than city life or that rural ideals are better than urban values. Paradoxically, this poem uses art to celebrate nature, thus reconciling implied opposites.

FORMALIST critics, who emphasize close, detailed readings of literature to determine how texts "work" as "works of art," might call particular attention, for instance, to the varied colors Kemp uses when she mentions gold, green, and silver in lines 7–10 and 17. They might also note the sheer variety of living things she mentions when describing the country, including grain, heifers, grass, and sheep (6–10), as well as trees, birds, and flowers (14–18). In contrast to nature's beautiful sights and sounds and attractive living things, she later mentions smoking streets, howling cries, and choking, infectious air when describing the city (25–8). Vivid imagery emphasizes the poem's implied and explicit themes, contributing to the artistry formalists admire.

PSYCHOANALYTIC critics are most interested in psychological complexities, whether of writer, character, speaker, or readers. Sometimes (especially if they are Lacanians) they also compare texts themselves to psyches or minds. What a text leaves left unsaid, for instance, is often as important as anything it openly articulates, just as the unconscious is often the most fascinating part of the mind. Psychoanalytic critics might argue that the Freudian id (the unconscious seat of fears and the yearning for pleasure) is especially emphasized in this poem. It celebrates the sensual pleasures of the countryside and implies fear of the discomforts and pain associated with the city. If we knew anything at all about Kemp we might be able to partly explain the poem by assessing her own psyche.

ARCHETYPAL critics, who emphasize common human responses to common stimuli, might argue that most human beings, everywhere, are and have always been attracted to natural beauty. Most humans probably resent being cramped into cities if those cities seem dark, confining, dirty, and unhealthy. The existence of parks suggests that even when humans live in urban areas they desire contact with nature. Most humans also prefer pleasant smells to stench; pleasant sounds to annoying noise; and pleasant sights to ugliness. Kemp's poem, therefore, arguably plays on deep-seated human instincts.

MARXIST critics, interested in improving conditions for the poor by promoting social and economic equality, might consider Kemp's poem ultimately disappointing. It does emphasize rural beauty but says almost nothing about the actual living conditions of the rural poor. The only rural person mentioned owns prized sheep, showing that he "is *not* poore" (10; emphasis added). When Kemp later laments the living conditions of urban dwellers, she does not single out the poor, nor does she propose any practical socioeconomic improvements. Instead, she merely anticipates the nostalgia she will feel for the country when she returns to the city. Her poem (Marxists might argue) suggests no real-world solutions to the problems it describes, nor does it put the blame for those problems where the blame belongs.

FEMINIST critics would welcome attention to a previously little-known text by a previously unknown woman writer. One main function of much feminist criticism is precisely to uncover and/or recover such texts. Kemp seems to have been an educated woman with strong opinions that she openly expressed. Yet the poem never reveals her full identity; we think she was the author only because someone happened to identify her on the poem's lone surviving copy. When Kemp wrote, there was still a widespread social prejudice against women being readily identifiable authors, especially in print. The mere fact that she used her initials rather than her name implies this prejudice.

STRUCTURALIST critics would note the many codes Kemp's poem implies. Knowledge of these codes (they would argue) is crucial to proper interpretation of this text. One code involves familiarity with classical culture. Anyone ignorant of the classics would be confused by the references to "Apelles" (1), "Elizium" (2), "Ceres" (7), "Lethe Lake" (12), and so on. Kemp knew this code and assumes that most of her readers will also know it. But the poem reflects many other codes, most of them grounded in binary opposites. These include country versus city, beauty versus ugliness, nature versus the unnatural; and, by implication, beautiful creations made by God versus the flawed, disappointing creations of fallen humans.

DECONSTRUCTIVE critics would look for any evidence suggesting that the neat interpretive categories proposed by structuralists (and most other kinds of interpreters) are wobbly and unstable. Thus the implied contrast between nature and civilization is undermined almost immediately when nature is described using terms borrowed from classical literature. Nature is not perceived freshly and objectively, with an "innocent eye"; rather, perceptions of nature are "always already" affected and even infected by the way one has been educated. Access to "nature," pure and simple, is never itself simple and pure; there is no straightforward, unmediated access to nature or "the natural." Nature and culture, apparent opposites, can never be clearly distinguished, nor can the simple distinction implying that the city is bad while the country is good be easily maintained. Only by excluding all the negative aspects of the countryside (such as droughts, disease, dangerous creatures, etc.) can Kemp maintain the distinctions she tries to establish—distinctions that would seem, to deconstructors, inherently infirm.

READER-RESPONSE critics would be open to most (perhaps all) imaginable responses to this poem. They would feel no need to choose one as the "best" or "correct" response. They would assume that responses to the poem would vary widely based on personal values and experiences. A city-lover, for instance, might think the poem unfairly presents urban life, which can be exciting and stimulating. Country folk might argue either (a) that country life is every bit as beautiful as Kemp suggests, or (b) that country life is far more tedious and boring than Kemp allows. Persons unfamiliar with (and uninterested in) classical culture might find the classical allusions pretentious and stuffy; persons deeply versed in classical culture might find those allusions resonant and stimulating, suggesting a continuity between the remote past and the speaker's present. In short, reader-response critics would suggest that there is no way to predict or regulate how readers might respond to Kemp's poem.

DIALOGICAL critics would note all the various tones and voices audible in this poem and all the different ways the poem is "in dialogue" with other writings. Clearly it alludes to numerous classical texts. All the classical references imply an educated speaker addressing an educated audience. Her classical knowledge helps "authorize" her text, giving it (in her culture) greater interest and legitimacy, especially since she is a woman writer. The switch, near the end, from celebrating the country to satirizing the city would also interest dialogical critics. It involves a shift from one tone to another, while the closing allusions to *Hamlet* put Kemp's poem "in dialogue" with yet another writer and text. Somewhat surprisingly, Kemp engages in no very obvious dialogue with the Christian Bible, the one text almost everyone in her culture would have known quite well.

NEW HISTORICIST critics might explore the ways Kemp's poem suggests various cultural tensions and conflicts of her era. The most obvious tension here is between the country and the city. London had become one of the largest cities in Europe and was only continuing to expand, not only in area and population but also in cultural influence. Rural areas and smaller towns were becoming less and less important, especially since more and more powerful people had residences there and chose to spend more and more of their time in London. During the reign of King James I, proclamations urged aristocrats and other wealthy people to spend more time in the countryside and fulfill their duties there, rather than luxuriating in the capital. Kemp, of course, mentions no urban pleasures. She makes city life sound utterly appalling. She thereby arguably falsifies her accounts of both country *and* city, failing to explain why people would want to abandon rural life and subject themselves to the noise, ugliness, stink, and disease of cities. The poem, then, is partly a political text: it contributes to an on-going debate rather than presenting a studiously objective account (if objective accounts of anything are even possible).

MULTICULTURALIST critics might note the various kinds of cultures implied in Kemp's poem, including classical, rural, urban, and specifically English. The poem is one of many texts celebrating rural England. The allusions to classical literature imply an appeal to figuratively "cultured" people who had been educated in the classics and who could see continuities between English and ancient cultures. Perhaps deliberately, there are no references to any subcultures within English society at the time: no references to Catholics or Protestants, to different *kinds* of Protestants, to men or women, to rich or poor, etc. Instead, the poem arguably ignores or erases multicultural differences that might have complicated or obscured its relatively simple, perhaps even simplistic contrast between the country and the city.

POSTMODERNIST critics might find Kemp's poem fairly unremarkable. It displays little of the inventiveness, ambiguity, incoherence, or randomness they tend to value. It could hardly be called experimental or cutting-edge. Its message is not particularly startling, and its classical allusions heighten its stylistic conservatism. It challenges no standard orthodoxies, and it does not seem especially open to multiple or conflicting interpretations. It is, in short, not the kind of work that would probably interest most postmodernists.

ECOCRITICS might be especially interested in Kemp's poem. After all, it celebrates the beauties of nature, denigrates human corruption of the environment, and lovingly describes natural landscapes, flora, and fauna. Humans are barely mentioned, but the poem does suggest that rural folk harmoniously coexist with nature. They raise crops and sheep, and nothing explicitly implies hunting or slaughter. The poem might be more satisfying to ecocritics if it showed people interacting more with nature and taking active efforts either to nurture nature or to repair the damage wrought in and by cities. (London was horribly polluted.) Nevertheless, Kemp's poem is intriguing, from an ecocritical perspective, as an unusually early, almost "pre-Romantic" hymn to natural beauty.

DARWINIAN critics might be able to explain why, precisely, most humans might find Kemp's vision of nature so appealing (as archetypal critics claim). According to many Darwinian theorists, humans flourished best and longest as a species in grassy lands bordering water with trees nearby but not in any great abundance.

These savannah areas provided many basic necessities of survival. The humans who were born and bred and who survived and reproduced in such areas were the ones who most often passed their genes on to the next generation. Thus humans (according to many Darwinians) find such areas innately attractive and would therefore find Kemp's poem appealing.

As the preceding thumbnail analyses have suggested, Kemp's poem, like almost any literary text, invites numerous kinds of comments from many different perspectives. Pluralists would suggest that no single theory is ever adequate to explaining all there is to explain in a complex work of literature. The best approach to literature (pluralists would maintain) is an approach that is open to many different points of view, some of them contradictory, many of them complementary, but all of them, ideally, capable of provoking thought, understanding, and even appreciation.

APPENDIX: THE KINDS OF QUESTIONS DIFFERENT CRITICS ASK

Christina M. Garner

The following lists of questions are derived from Robert C. Evans's book *Close Readings* and are designed to give students and other readers a practical series of questions to ask of any literary work as they try to make sense of its phrasing, structures, and meanings.

Plato

How does the work

- reflect enduring reality?
- appeal to the reader either mainly logically (which is good) or mainly emotionally (which is bad)?
- attempt (successfully or unsuccessfully) to influence society?
- ask and/or answer philosophical questions?
- stress subject matter and content as opposed to form and craftsmanship?
- utilize logic or reason rather than emotional or sensory stimuli to explore truth?
- convey ideas about absolute truth and beauty?
- help readers discover philosophical truths?

- inform or instruct rather than simply entertain?
- seem objective, rational, and systematic?
- attempt to make reason and virtue attractive?
- endorse or undermine truth?

Aristotle

How does the work

- suggest or reveal enduring truth?
- demonstrate conscious, deliberate craftsmanship?
- reflect the writer's skill in using a particular genre (or kind) of writing?
- reflect any general insight into human nature, thoughts, and actions?
- combine unity and complexity, especially in relations between its various parts?
- imply natural, inevitable, consistent connections between different parts of the work?
- reflect some natural, necessary way of ordering or understanding experience (such as tragic experience or comic experience)?
- help satisfy an innate, inevitable human desire for knowledge?
- reveal how individual experience reflects larger truths?
- reflect the existence of a general human nature?
- provoke general, typical human responses rather than idiosyncratic ones?
- provoke responses to both its form and its content, which are inseparable?
- reveal the dynamic forms, patterns, or processes inherent in reality?
- reveal the way a thing can change while still remaining the same thing?

- help us discover truths about reality, both external and internal?
- help us understand meaningful patterns of human behavior?
- lend itself to objective, rational, and systematic examination?
- seem valuable as an imitation of reality?

Horace

How does the work

- reflect or respond to the preferences of its intended audience?
- adhere to or depart from the requirements of a particular genre?
- reflect literary traditions or customs?
- make each character look or act in ways that are appropriate or expected for that character? (For example, how does an old, male character look or act like a stereotypical old man?)
- connect events in the text in ways that seem natural or expected?
- balance simplicity and complexity and seem consistent?
- utilize or fail to utilize language which is familiar to the reader?
- reflect real life, especially by presenting characters who seem realistic or credible?
- reflect the deliberate craftsmanship of the writer?
- instruct and/or entertain the reader?
- appeal to a broad audience?
- meet or violate the reader's expectations?
- imply the values, customs, and conventions of its intended audience?
- reflect any general insight into human nature?
- reflect the ways that conventions and audiences change over time?

Longinus

How does the work

- demonstrate the writer's conscious, deliberate craftsmanship?
- reflect the character of the writer?
- display the writer's genius or inspiration?
- convey sublime spiritual, moral, and/or intellectual power?
- inspire artistic or ethical achievement in others?
- reflect the fact that humanity is capable of producing great, powerful works?
- display noble ideas or elevated language?
- achieve unity and harmony?
- reveal the author reflecting or building upon the skill of his/her predecessors?
- emphasize spiritual and ethical greatness as opposed to triviality or materialism?
- reveal the shared human nature and fundamental desires that people possess?
- use rhetorical devices (such as metaphor, simile, etc.)?
- encourage noble aspirations?
- transcend the boundaries of class, gender, race, nation, and time to appeal to a wide variety of readers?

Traditional historical criticism

How does the work

- reflect the writer's values?
- reflect the values of a particular historical era?
- reflect the author's individual experiences?
- become more comprehensible the more we know about the era in which it was written?
- give us insights into the period in which it was written?
- reveal the influence of previous texts?

- become more comprehensible the more we understand the language of its era?
- seem open to different interpretations in different historical eras?
- seem affected by the society in which it was produced?
- influence the society in which it was produced?

Thematic criticism

How does the work

- intentionally or unintentionally incorporate abstract ideas?
- use abstract ideas or concepts to convey meaning?
- imply the beliefs and values of its author?
- repeat or reflect ideas emphasized in other works by its author?
- imply that ideas are important aspects of reality?
- reflect any general insight into human nature?
- reflect any larger truths about existence or the nature of the world?
- repeatedly emphasize one central theme or motif?
- provoke thoughts about abstract ideas?
- focus on ideas rather than on details of phrasing or structure?
- use one or more idea to convey the overall message or meaning of the text?
- use general ideas to make sense of particular details of the work?
- rely on the human desire or need to understand experiences in terms of large, meaningful patterns or ideas?
- emphasize broad, familiar ideas (e.g., good vs. evil; right vs. wrong; the purpose of living; the nature of happiness; fate vs. free will; war and peace; crime and punishment; the nature of love, or of justice, or of duty, or of truth)?
- convey lessons about and/or insights into the ideas it explores?

Formalism

How does the work

- attempt to reveal truth?
- reflect the writer's skill in the use of a particular genre (or kind) of writing?
- demonstrate conscious, deliberate craftsmanship?
- exhibit complex unity, so that every part of the work is necessary to the work as a whole?
- reveal connections between different parts of the work that seem natural and inevitable?
- reflect, through its own complexity, the complexity of reality?
- provoke responses both to its form and to its content (which are inseparable)?
- suggest the dynamic forms, patterns, or processes inherent in reality?
- help us understand meaningful patterns of human behavior?

Psychoanalytic criticism

How does the work

- suggest the unconscious drives or motives of the writer, the reader, and/or the works' characters?
- reveal the influences of the writer's unconscious mind?
- suggest the interaction of the *id* (the subconscious, instinctual, pleasure-seeking mind), the *ego* (the conscious, rational mind), and the *superego* (the conscience), either in the writer, the reader, and/or the work's characters?
- imply repression (especially sexual repression) of the *id*, either in the writer, the reader, and/or the work's characters?
- suggest or reveal larger truths about various stages of human development?

- imply or express ideas about psychosexual or gender roles?
- imply or present a writer and/or characters who express highly individual or personal psychological realities?
- imply the collective psychology of society during the writer's lifetime?

Archetypal criticism

How does the work

- appeal to thoughts and feelings that almost all readers share?
- provoke general, typical human responses rather than idiosyncratic reactions?
- reveal multiple levels of complexity and psychological significance?
- reveal both a surface meaning and an underlying level of meaning which is, in many cases, more important than the surface meaning?
- use patterns of imagery or themes that provoke the same responses in most people?
- imply the existence of a general human nature?
- use general human associations to imply deeper meanings (e.g., by using darkness to suggest danger or springtime to symbolize life or rebirth)?
- explore the relationships between humans and nature?
- disclose underlying patterns that contribute to the text's deeper unity or coherence?
- use symbols that can have multiple meanings depending on their contexts?
- appeal to readers' most basic desires, needs?
- appeal to readers emotionally or psychologically rather than intellectually?
- transcend barriers of age, race, language, gender, and so on to appeal to a more universal human nature?

- resemble many other texts in its underlying meanings and impact?
- employ patterns or symbols also found in popular literature?
- imply universal feelings or responses that are typically very important or powerful and, therefore, very difficult to put into words?
- use symbols, themes, or ideas appropriate to the text's genre?
- manipulate characters, symbols, or themes to uphold or undermine the reader's expectations?

Marxist criticism

How does the work

- reflect the writer's socioeconomic circumstances?
- reflect its own social or historical contexts?
- depict or deal with the social structure that helped produce it? (For instance, does the work describe, distort, falsify, criticize, or endorse the social structure, or does it do some combination of these things?)
- reveal the distribution of power within the social structure?
- strengthen or weaken the interests of a particular economic class?
- reveal anything about power struggles or injustices within or between social classes?
- reveal how the dominant class uses "spiritual" or "natural" practices to maintain dominance?
- deal with values or systems of belief that stifle or weaken progress for the majority?
- reveal the social and/or political agenda(s) the characters and/or writer support?
- support or oppose the dominant ideology of its time?
- provoke different potential reactions in readers of different economic classes?
- challenge individual readers or society as a whole?

Feminist criticism

How does the work

- reflect the assumptions the writer or his/her culture makes about sexuality and gender?
- accept and/or reject prevailing assumptions about sexuality and gender?
- reflect the impact of the writer's gender or sexual identity?
- reflect and/or reject the sexual or gender stereotypes of the writer's culture?
- influence the sexual or gender stereotypes of the writer's culture?
- challenge and/or affirm the sexual or gender identities of audience members?
- show characters within the text behaving in terms of their gender identities?
- show characters upholding or challenging society's assumptions about gender and/or sexuality?
- promote or stifle social progress or individual freedoms, especially freedoms relevant to sexuality and/or gender?

Structuralist criticism

How does the work

- use particular codes or structured languages?
- reveal anything about the codes or structures that people use to understand the world around them?
- suggest that codes change in different cultures or time periods?
- use opposites (such as good vs. evil, light vs. dark, young vs. old, etc.) to reveal meaning within the text?
- adhere to or depart from the rules or codes of its genre (or kind) of writing?
- use specific words or ideas that reveal or imply the codes that govern the text?

- present characters who abide by or oppose the codes within the text?
- seem consistent or inconsistent in its use of codes or structures?
- use codes or structures that allow a reader to understand the meaning of the text more deeply or completely?
- use overlapping codes or structures?

Deconstructionism

How does the work

- employ particular codes or structured languages?
- reveal that the codes or structures that govern the text are full of contradictions, inconsistencies, or even paradoxes?
- lack unity or patterns of consistent meaning?
- suggest that it is *readers* who impose structures on the text in order to find meaning within the text?
- imply anything about the codes or structures that people use to understand the world around them, especially the inconsistencies of those codes?
- reflect but also violate the rules of a particular genre?
- reveal parts that seem inconsistent with the text as a whole?
- seem consistent and/or especially *inconsistent* in its use of codes or structures?
- seem unsuccessful in depicting an objective reality?
- undermine readers' expectations or assumptions about reality?

Reader-response criticism

How does the work

- seem subject to the reader's control rather than controlling the reader?
- seem open to different interpretations by different readers or different kinds of readers?

- reveal that the author's control over the text is limited?
- suggest anything about different readers' differing perceptions of reality?

Dialogical criticism

How does the work

- show the effects of having been written for an intended audience, so that the text is in a kind of dialogue with its potential readers?
- seem focused on affecting its intended audience, so that the text seems shaped with this audience in mind?
- present literal or figurative dialogue within the text, as when characters speak to each other, or different styles seem to interact, or different worldviews interact?
- present individual voices in the text (whether those of the writer or those of the characters) that represent the interests, beliefs, or thoughts of multiple points of view?
- communicate, or seem engaged in a dialogue, with other texts?
- allude to or quote another text? How does any such reference affect the text's meaning or the ways readers interpret the text?
- use first-, second-, and/or third-person narration throughout the text?
- use different kinds of narrative points of view, such as omniscient or limited perspectives?
- use points of view that communicate with or represent various points of view in society?
- imply meaningful relationships between what the text says and what it leaves unsaid?

New historicism

How does the work

- suggest that it and/or its author are affected by multiple, even contradictory, influences?

- reveal highly complex historical contexts (plural)?
- seem affected by contemporary social forces while also trying to affect society?
- seem an active historical force rather than a passive product of historical influence?
- seem especially meaningful when read in light of other texts from its historical period, even (or especially) texts that do not seem immediately or obviously relevant?
- seem affected by diverse, conflicting, or unstable ideologies rather than a single, unified ideology?
- provoke complicated, conflicting, or unstable reactions from readers?
- suggest that the popular view of a historical event (such as the view presented in a history textbook) is not the only view or even the most accurate view?
- suggest that an individual's experience of reality is influenced by multiple forces?
- suggest that one individual's experience of reality may contradict another individual's experience of reality?
- suggest the numerous, often conflicting interests of individuals in a society?
- about relations of power and how those power relations change?
- explore historical figures or events in new or unusual ways?

Multiculturalism

How does the work

- reflect the fact that the writer is a member of multiple, often overlapping cultural groups? (Cultural groups can center on a nearly infinite number of values or characteristics. Some examples are race, sexual identity, nationality, age, gender, height, hair color, education level, religious affiliation, political affiliation.)
- reflect the influence of the groups to which the writer belongs?

- reveal anything about the writer's experiences as a member of a group or groups?
- appeal to readers as members of multiple, often overlapping cultural groups?
- seem open to different interpretations by members of different groups?
- present characters who seem to be members of multiple, often overlapping cultural groups?
- present characters who seem affected by their memberships in particular groups?
- suggest that a truly neutral or objective interpretation of the text may be impossible?
- suggest that each person experiences reality differently from every other person, partly because each person belongs to particular groups?
- suggest that a general "human nature" does not exist?
- explore—or attempt to ignore—human differences?
- either affirm and/or undermine the values or social powers of a cultural group or groups?
- reflect relations (often tense relations) between a dominant culture and a less powerful culture?
- reflect relations between a colonial power and a culture that is (or was once) colonized?

Postmodernism

How does the work

- explore multiple positions, roles, attitudes, or stances (for the writer, reader, and/or characters) within the work?
- seem complex, ambiguous, or even contradictory?
- suggest that incoherencies or chaos in the text represent a degree of freedom?
- interact with and appropriate popular culture?

- suggest that popular culture is in a constant state of change?
- blur the lines between "high" and "low" art?
- reveal internal gaps, inconsistencies, or randomness?
- mix, juxtapose, and/or combine varying genres?
- adhere to and/or depart from the traditional rules of traditional genre(s)?
- implicitly or explicitly reject the existence of a coherent, unified reality?
- seem to undermine or subvert systems of belief, ideologies, worldviews, logic, or reason?
- seem playful or ironic?
- implicitly or explicitly challenge ideologies (such as Marxism, structuralism, Christianity, Freudianism, etc.) that try to make sense of or impose order on the text or the world?
- emphasize surface meaning over the existence of some deep, underlying meaning?
- use elements that seem ornamental, decorative, or illusory?
- seem open to multiple, often contradictory interpretations?
- seem to lack any absolute, stable significance?

Ecocriticism

How does the work

- emphasize relationships between humans and nature, especially relations with other animals as well as plants, but also including the physical environment?
- reveal the ways that humans often misuse or exploit the rest of "nature" (in all the various senses of that term)?
- implicitly (and ideally) oppose human misuse of nature, especially other living things?
- appeal to deeply rooted human love of nature and/or appeal to humans' sense of self-interest in being good stewards of nature?

Darwinian criticism

How does the work

- imply the existence of a general human nature resulting from millions of years of evolution?

- reflect and appeal to general psychological traits that have evolved over millions of years?

- suggest a general human artistic desire to make things "special" (or make "special things")?

- reflect the fact that the author is a human speaking to other humans in ways they will enjoy or comprehend because both author and audience share the same evolutionary past?

- reflect a basic human tendency to tell the same basic stories repeatedly and to find those basic stories continually relevant or interesting?

- imply relations between humans and nature that reflect millions of years of evolution?

- reflect or promote patterns of thinking and/or behavior that promote evolutionary "fitness," including the passing on of genes from one generation to the next?

Table 1 *An "Abrams scheme" of various literary theories*

	Writer	Text	Audience	Reality	Critic
Plato	imitates mere appearances; has no real knowledge	inaccurately reflects reality; thus typically offers false views of reality	likely to be emotional, irrational, and thus easily deceived	can (and must) be known objectively through use of reason and logic	should use reason to make judgments and should act as monitor
Aristotle	skilled craftsman capable of true knowledge	complexly unified work of art that can communicate truth	capable of appreciating craft; eager to learn	reality is complex and can be grasped in various ways	a specialist who knows the details of poetic craft
Horace	seeks to satisfy a diverse audience	should follow custom and moderation	teaching and/or pleasing a broad audience is crucial	is understood in traditional or conventional terms	a fatherly advisor who helps poets avoid mistakes
Longinus	lofty, noble, inspired genius	expresses power of the author's soul	seeks elevation, ecstasy, nobility	human nature seeks elevation	spiritual advisor to poet, audience
Traditional historical criticism	is embedded in a particular historical era	reflects the ideas and circumstances of its time	respond in ways typical of their historical period	social realities differ during different periods	must possess thorough historical knowledge
Thematic criticism	expresses (often-recurring) ideas	interesting largely for its ideas	interested in ideas that texts express	ideas help shape social reality	studies ideas embedded in texts
Formalist criticism	highly skilled craftsman	richly complex unity	interested in subtle artistry	reality itself tends to be complex	closely analyzes text's complex unity and subtlety

Psychoanalytic criticism	torn between id, ego, superego	reflects conflicts in minds of writer and audience	respond according to individual "identity themes"	individual mental (especially unconscious) reality is crucial	must know human psychological complexities
Archetypal criticism	deeply affected by basic human fears, desires, and experiences	skillfully plays on basic human fears, desires, stories, symbols	compulsively respond to basic desires, fears, stories, symbols	all people share certain basic desires and fears (i.e., a basic human nature)	should study the impact of basic emotions, stories, images, events
Marxist criticism	inevitably affected by economic class conflicts, whether consciously or not	reflects, reinforces, and/or undermines interests of the dominant class	divided by economic class interests, whether they are aware of these or not	dominant ideas of society reflect economic divisions and conflicts in society	should study the complex relations between literature and society to promote progress
Structuralist criticism	must rely on codes commonly used within the culture to create and convey meaning	inevitably reflects the structures and (binary) codes of its society; e.g. red light vs. green light	use cultural codes and structures—especially language—to interpret anything	humans make sense of reality by imposing structures or codes (e.g., words) on it	must be deeply familiar with the actual codes and structures specific texts reflect

Table 1 *Continued*

	Writer	Text	Audience	Reality	Critic
Feminist criticism	is inevitably affected by society's gender categories, especially the category of "male" vs. "female"	either reflects, reaffirms, and/or undermines society's gender categories; ideally questions them	experience reality in terms of gender categories, which often repress women	experience is structured by gender categories, especially the categories of "male" vs. "female"	should know society's assumptions about gender and challenge them if they are repressive
Deconstructive criticism	can never impose complete or perfect control over any text	is inevitably full of irresolvable contradictions and paradoxes	can never escape the contradictions texts embody; should therefore accept them	"reality" can only be experienced through codes that are full of gaps and contradictions	searches out the contradictory, paradoxical aspects of texts that prevent unity
Reader-response criticism	cannot really control how any audience responds to his/her text	each text will provoke a unique response in each audience	different audiences or persons respond differently to the same texts	each reader or group of readers will perceive reality in a distinctive way	must take into account the actual responses of varied audiences

Dialogical criticism	must be aware of, and capable of using, different voices and thereby engage in dialogue with audience and other texts	the best texts reflect more than one voice, tone, or point of view; these are often in dialogue, and the text is often in dialogue with its audience and with other texts	the complex nature of the audience will be reflected in divergent tones and voices within the text	can (and will) be perceived from different points of view; the richest texts reflect these differences	the sensitive critic must be alert to the multitude of voices or tones a text expresses or implies and the different kinds of dialogues in which a text participates
New historicist criticism	is embedded in a highly complex culture and cannot help reflecting the tensions inherent therein	the text will reflect, and take part in, the constant negotiation, exchange, and struggle for power	is composed of individuals and groups whose status is complex and constantly in flux	our experience of reality is inevitably social and reflects the struggle for power; any culture is a site of conflict	must be aware of the ways historical circumstances affected past texts and how they affect her own
Multicultural criticism	inevitably is a member of a group or groups and cannot escape this fact	will provoke different kinds of responses from different groups	inevitably belong to a group or groups and respond accordingly	numerous group differences shape and divide social reality	must be aware of the impact of group differences on the writing and reading of texts

Table 1 *Continued*

	Writer	Text	Audience	Reality	Critic
Postmodernist criticism	can never impose order or control on the text and therefore should be open to all kinds of influences	the best texts are the ones that revel in their contradictions, complexities, and randomness	should give up their old-fashioned yearning for order and coherence and enjoy the fluidity of texts	"reality" is so complex and chaotic that no explanation of it can ever be final or perfect	should doubt any "grand explanations" and celebrate the instabilities inherent in any text
Ecocriticism	should write in ways that reveal human abuse of nature and should promote responsible attitudes toward the environment and other living things	will reflect in various ways the relationship between humans and nature, especially any human misuse or abuse of nature	should be interested in, or be willing to be interested in, responsible human behavior toward nature	is primarily physical and material; the health of the natural environment and ecosystem is crucial to healthy human existence	should examine works to see the ways they depict nature (including other creatures) and whether those depictions promote ecological responsibility

| Darwinian criticism | will tend to write in ways that reflect the shared psychological traits of humans—traits that have evolved over millions of years | will reflect (in such matters as imagery, plot, themes, and characterization) the interests, fears, desires, and other traits that humans share as a result of millions of years of evolution | consists of people whose similarities—especially in ways of thinking, feeling, perceiving, and reacting—have evolved over the course of millions of years. These basic biological and psychological similarities are far more important than individual or cultural differences | is primarily physical, material, and biological and particularly involves human interaction with the environment in a quest to survive and physically reproduce | should be alert to the ways basic biological impulses (such as the impulses to survive, reproduce, and gain and maintain status) affect the writing and reading of literature and the ways literature presents characters and appeals to people |

BIBLIOGRAPHY

Abrams, M. H. *The Mirror and the Lamp: Romantic Theory and the Critical Tradition.* Oxford: Oxford University Press, 1953.

Aristotle. "Poetics." Trans. S. H. Butcher. In Bate 19–39.

Bate, Walter Jackson. *Criticism: The Major Texts.* Enlarged edn. New York: Harcourt Brace Jovanovich, 1970.

Brumble, H. David. *Classical Myths and Legends in the Middle Ages and Renaissance: A Dictionary of Allegorical Meanings.* Westport, CT: Greenwood, 1998.

Brumble, H. David. "John Donne's 'The Flea': Some Implications of the Encyclopedic and Poetic Flea Traditions." *Critical Quarterly* 15.2 (1973): 147–54.

Dawson, Terence and Robert Scott Dupree, eds., *Seventeenth Century English Poetry: The Annotated Anthology.* London: Harvester Wheatsheaf, 1994.

Horace. "Art of Poetry." Trans. Walter Jackson Bate. In Bate 51–8.

Longinus. Excerpts from "On the Sublime." Trans. W. Rhys Roberts. In Bate 62–75.

Longinus. "On Sublimity." Trans. D. A. Russell. In Preminger et al. 192–225.

Marvell, Andrew. *The Poems.* Ed. Nigel Smith. Rev. edn. London: Routledge, 2006.

Plato. Excerpts from *Ion* and *The Republic.* Trans. Benjamin Jowett. In Bate 43–9.

Plato. Excerpts from *The Symposium, Phaedrus, Gorgias, Ion,* Books III of *The Republic,* Book X of *The Republic,* and Book VII of *Laws.* In Preminger et al. 25–96.

Preminger, Alex, O. B. Hardison, and Kevin Kerrane. *Classical and Medieval Literary Criticism: Translations and Interpretations.* New York: Unger, 1974.

FURTHER READING

The present book, which is mainly concerned with applying literary theories to various texts, is an outgrowth of several previous studies that explore and explain literary theories in some detail while also offering many specific applications of them. Those studies include the following:

Evans, Robert C. *Ambrose Bierce's "An Occurrence at Owl Creek Bridge": An Annotated Critical Edition*. West Cornwall: Locust Hill, 2003. [Freely available online.]

Evans, Robert C. *Close Readings: Analyses of Short Fiction from Multiple Perspectives*. 3rd edn. Montgomery: NewSouth, 2010.

Evans, Robert C. *Frank O'Connor's "Ghosts": A Pluralist Approach*. Montgomery: Court Street, 2003.

Evans, Robert C. *Kate Chopin's Short Fiction: A Critical Companion*. West Cornwall: Locust Hill, 2001.

Evans, Robert C. *Perspectives on World War I Poetry*. London: Bloomsbury, 2014.

The studies listed below offer full, accessible explanations of the theories discussed in the present book.

Bressler, Charles E. *Literary Criticism: An Introduction to Theory and Practice*. 5th edn. Boston: Longman, 2011.

Dobie, Ann B. *Theory into Practice: An Introduction to Literary Criticism*. 3rd edn. Boston: Wadsworth, 2012.

Guerin, Wilfred L., Earle Labor, Lee Morgan, Jeanne C. Reesman, and John R. Willingham. *A Handbook of Critical Approaches to Literature*. 6th edn. Oxford: Oxford University Press, 2011.

Parker, Robert D. *How to Interpret Literature: Critical Theory for Literary and Cultural Studies*. 2nd edn. Oxford: Oxford University Press, 2011.

Tyson, Lois. *Critical Theory Today: A User-Friendly Guide*. 2nd edn. New York: Routledge, 2006.

The anthologies listed below offer access to many important primary texts associated with the theories discussed in this book:

Adams, Hazard and Leroy Searle, eds. *Critical Theory since Plato*. Boston: Thomson/Wadsworth, 2005.

Bate, Walter J. *Criticism: The Major Texts*. Enlarged edn. New York: Harcourt Brace Jovanovich, 1970.

Leitch, Vincent B. and William E. Cain, eds. *The Norton Anthology of Theory and Criticism*. New York: Norton, 2010.

Rivkin, Julie and Michael Ryan, eds. *Literary Theory: An Anthology*. Oxford: Blackwell, 2010.

Most of the poems discussed in this book are freely available on the internet, but useful printed anthologies include the following:

Black, Joseph et al., eds. *The Broadview Anthology of British Literature, Volume 2: The Renaissance and the Early Seventeenth Century*. Guelph, ON: Broadview, 2010.

Greenblatt, Stephen et al., eds. *The Norton Anthology of English Literature*, volume 1. 7th edn. New York: Norton, 2003.

Hunter, John C., ed. *Renaissance Literature: An Anthology of Poetry and Prose*. Oxford: Wiley-Blackwell, 2010.

INDEX OF THEORIES
AND APPLICATIONS